THE ELDER TREE

Memorabilia of a Traditional
Tyneside Family

The author in pensive mood

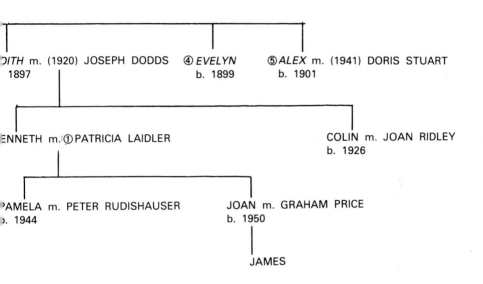

DITH m. (1920) JOSEPH DODDS   ④ EVELYN   ⑤ ALEX m. (1941) DORIS STUART
1897   b. 1899   b. 1901

ENNETH m. ① PATRICIA LAIDLER   COLIN m. JOAN RIDLEY
                                                      b. 1926

PAMELA m. PETER RUDISHAUSER   JOAN m. GRAHAM PRICE
). 1944   b. 1950

                                      JAMES

        KENNETH m. ② SHEILA WALKER

                RUTH
                b. 1968

THE WONDERFULL WOODS
OF CULBOKIE.

Now youre about to retire.
May the future hold all you
                    desire.
And for the new folks who
                    own.
Be they ROBINSON, SMITH
            BROWN OR JONES
They may fill all our village
            with ROODIES.
But our stars will be
always called
            "WOODYS".

FROM
Tom & Jesson Lildar.

THE ELDER TREE

Memorabilia of a Traditional Tyneside Family

THE PENTLAND PRESS LTD
EDINBURGH   CAMBRIDGE   DURHAM

First published in 1991 by
The Pentland Press Ltd.
Brockerscliffe
Witton le Wear
Durham

ISBN 1 872795 14 5

Typeset in 10pt Times by Print Origination (NW)
Limited, Formby, Liverpool L37 8EG
Printed and bound by Antony Rowe
Limited, Chippenham, Wiltshire SN14 6LH

CONTENTS

THE ROOTS OF THE ELDER TREE

FLOWERS AND FRUITS OF THE ELDER TREE

LIST OF ILLUSTRATIONS

DEDICATION

This book is dedicated to two of my sisters, Edith Dodds and Jennie Richardson, both of whom devoted the major part of their youth to a magnificent performance in the role of 'Little Mother' to our large family.

The Roots of the Elder Tree

The Romance of the Northland

When I was a lad of seven, I took a message to my father who was Check Weighman at the shaft of the Betty Pit at Teams Colliery in County Durham. I was most awed and frightened by the infernal clanging of iron tubs being heaved out of the cages – the whine of the engine – the roar of the coal screens – the clouds of dust as coal poured down shutes into waiting waggons – the shouting of black faced scurrying men; but most of all during a lull in the winding work my father took me to the mouth of that awful shaft and let me lean out until I saw the light at the bottom a quarter of a mile away.

It shook me to the core and though I visited pits since and travelled miles from the shaft bottom into the workings I have never worked in one.

The lesson I learned that day was deliberately given and received. At the age of sixteen I was having tea in an old terraced house in the pit village of Beamish. My host was Jack Lawson our local MP. It was Sunday evening and we were taken on the usual Sunday Evening walk through a copse called Yews Tops to a grassy knoll called the Money Hills where a band played.

'Why is it called the Money Hills, Mr Lawson?'

'It's an old legend about buried treasure; without foundation as far as we know' he said and went on, 'but you can find mystery and romance wherever you look, even across our battered county of Durham.'

He spread out his arms in a sweeping gesture over the tree tops. He had no need to point out the great black hills of colliery waste that marked our villages, however romantically named they might be.

Chester-le-Street, the Roman camp on the road, Fatfield, Pelton, the Felling where first trees were felled on the banks of the Tyne, Teams Colliery, Haswell, Blackfell and away above all, Shadons Hill three

3

fields from my home where once twenty thousand miners were confronted by the local coal owner Lord Durham with a detachment of cavalry.

Later at home, intrigued by the story of the copse I sent Mr Lawson my version of The Money Hills, finishing as you know, with his words 'The romance of the Northland'.

Years later and much wiser I walked through the Yew Tops of Beamish and stood again on the Money Hills, looking out on my ravaged homeland in the light of its history, to Fatfield where sixty nine men, women and boys were killed in one explosion; to the Felling where ninety two men and boys died in one night; to Haswell where in 1844 ninety six men and boys were lost; and just out of range the smoke still rises from Hartley where in 1862 two hundred and four lives were lost in an explosion. Between 1800 and 1836 nine hundred and eighty five miners were killed in County Durham alone.

In the year of Waterloo it is recorded that an Assize Judge said, and I quote: 'It is customary not to trouble about a coroner's inquest if the corpse is only that of a collier'.

Such was the land of my fathers in the last century.

And what of the mothers?

I quote, a pitman's wife:

'I go to bed only on Saturday nights. My husband and our three sons are all on different shifts and one or other of them is coming in or going out of the house, requiring a meal every three hours of the twenty four.'

The Money Hills

Come sit with me on yonder knoll
And listen while the streamlet trills,
And trips its track away below
Between the Money Hills

Such tales that brook could tell
Could she but pause and rest,
How from the hills she follows
Woody dimples where God's finger pressed.

How lurking in a hovel near his bank
The startled Briton glimpsed the shining rank
As Rome in jingling mail marched north
To bar the sturdy Scotsman's flank.

They came, they saw, they conquered,
Lived, fought and sounded the retreat,
And hurrying southward, so the legend goes,
They hid a treasure somewhere 'neath our feet.

And up yon brackened slope
Where rabbits squat
Great herds of Saxon swine once roamed
While Gurth the Swineherd sat this very spot.

All this yon brook has seen,
And heard the curfew's clang the valley fill;
As serf with toil-tired oxen
Climbed the brow of yonder hill.

And once some idiot prince in childish fit,
Cursed all the land with fire.
He died. The brook and time went on,
And nature blossomed from her funeral pyre.

A band of wandering monks
Pushed through the brake in search
Of quietness and stopped beside the brook
And built a Church.

They set the brook to turn a mill
Except on Holy Sabbath day.
On Thursday's Friars hooked the wily trout
To cheat the Friday of a meatless day.

They passed away. Perhaps yon mossgrown milldam
Is their only trace.
Time and the brook went on
And men grew up apace.

They forsook water's kindly aid
And turned to steam. They dug for coal amain.
The brook perhaps once wandered
And trickled down Dame Nature's vein.

She came up on the Underworld
Where Naked men dig buried power,
Under the wheels that raise it up
To fill the world with stoure.

They came in hundreds for the
Hidden sunshine Nature keeps.
They tore her treasure forth
And made great ugly heaps.

The ancient brown and mud walls that graced
Yon bank are gone. Instead,
Long rows of mud-brick houses stand.
The mud is baked bright red.

The collier's children now dip in the stream
And scramble through the copse;
While Sunday finds their elders on this knoll
While music fills the breeze through yon Yew Tops.

'And is there really treasure buried here?' you ask
'Or was it found by someone long ago?'
'Tis here for all who seek in the right spirit.
The brook will take your hand. Now off you go!

You can't? Then sit with me upon this knoll,
And listen while the streamlet trills
And trips its track away below,
Between the Money Hills.

Now cast your memory back down history's tale
And as the brook yon ancient pages fills.
The romance of our Northland springs to life.
You've found the treasure of the Money Hills.

Beamish Yew Tops 1927
Dedicated to Jack Lawson M.P.

Bloody Price of Coal

In 1885 a cage ascended to the mouth of the Betty Pit, Ravensworth, and out stepped my Grandfather, James Elder, and his son, James Elder, my father, aged 14 after his first day down the mine. Young Jim was tired, and his Dad gave him a piggy back, along the lane beyond Low Eighton through the White House Fields towards the Pontop and Jarrow Railway on which they were to hitch a lift home to Black Fell.

The coal waggons towed by endless rope, moved slowly through a cutting where it was easy to hoist young Jim onto the top of the coal.

As Grandpa made to join him he slipped and fell between the waggons. Here he was found four hours later having lost half a leg and half a hand. He survived by taking out the laces of his boots and putting a tourniquet on the arm and leg. He was taken by horse and cart five miles to Newcastle Infirmary and lived to a ripe old age producing a son well after the age of sixty, who lost a leg in the pit when a teenager.

My favourite memory of that grand old man was seeing him stamping up his garden using his wooden leg as a dibber with his wife planting potatoes in his wake.

My Grandsire stood astraddle
One leg of solid beech,
My Uncle leaned the other way
They bought but one shoe each.
A tale this not for laughter
However badly told,
A true tale of my boyhood
The bloody price of coal.

A ton will cost you twenty quid
Delivered to your hob.
Fifty years ago today

'Twas more like twenty bob.
Up in Durham coal field
All along the Tyne,
Miner's bones as cheap as stones
The land of me and mine.

A pitman's life was rough and tough
His wife's was even worse,
She had to back her menfolk
From a very shallow purse.
How would you set about and feed
A family of ten?
You had to stint your young 'uns
'Cause you couldn't stint your men.

Ungodly hours of the night
A man goes to the pit,
His woman's work to see him go
Dry clothed and full and fit.
A flannel shirt worn next his skin
To hold and soak the sweat,
His hob nailed shoes with dripping shine
Because he's working wet.

He pats his pocket on the left,
His bait of bread and jam
An old tin bottle in the right,
Cold tea his thirst to dam.
The ritual is near complete
But ere he's on his way
He takes and gives a kiss
That whispers, 'I'll be back today.'

Black stranger from the pithead,
Bad omen in the row,
And every curtain hears a prayer
That past this door he'll go.
Once past each house, its people
Come silent from their hiding
To see on whose door he shall knock
Black man with evil tidings!

From this grew a tradition
Black men never roam,
And knock not on another's door
Till that wife's man is home.
My Father was a teller,
The friend who'd get there first,
The man to look into that face
And watch it guess the worst.

One day I looked up at the gate
And saw three figures black,
The middle one was dad
I saw his leg kept dragging back.
I called and ran, he gripped my mouth,
One finger on his lips,
The mangled foot held off the ground
I watched the scarlet drips.

They leaned him on the corner wall,
And left, 'A'll be aall r'eet.'
The black men stopped and watched him
From the gate into the street.
He peered toward the door
And there she stood still unalarmed.
He screamed, 'I'm alright, Hinney,'
And launched into her arms.

My Grandsire stood astraddle
One leg of solid beech,
My Uncle leaned the other way
They bought but one shoe each.
Up in Durham coal field
All along the Tyne,
Miner's bones as cheap as stones
The land of me and mine.

March 7th. 1972.

My Earliest Memory

I have always been noted for my vivid memory, and consequently it was a great blow to me when recently I found my powers of recollection fading. Far from being unable to recall even recent happenings I was so perturbed at these mental blackouts that I sought out a psychiatrist and put my problem to him.

'How long has this been going on?' he asked.

'How long has what been going on?' I replied.

For some reason he began to lose his temper and after asking me to touch my toes he sneaked up and gave me a hefty kick in the subconscious.

When I came out of hospital, I found my powers of recollection fully restored except for one lapse – I could not for the life of me remember to pay the consultant's fee.

Ah yes. Where was I?

Oh Yes! My earliest memory. Sorry to keep you waiting.

I have in fact many vivid memories of the days before I was born, which I have been requested by my family to reserve for my ultimate memoirs.

This request apart, I will now proceed to recount my first impression of life on this planet.

Human babies have been born in all manner of situations: in carriages, buses, at sea, in the street and, of course, some in palaces. I was born in a little miner's cottage in the North, principally because I wanted to be near my mother at the time.

I was born on April the First, an apparently inauspicious date, arranged by my parents some time earlier.

Unfortunately at this time, there was much industrial unrest in the North and the NUM was on strike, and owing to the irascibility of certain shop stewards of the National Union of Mineworkers, they were not content until they had called out the National Union of Midwives.

Apparently my mother's appeal for help at the confinement was channelled to the wrong union and she was rather taken aback when a masked official demanded to know which party she was in.

'This is no party', she answered, 'I'm in labour!'.

'That's OK,' came the reply, 'We'll send somebody around'.

I suppose I was one of the first babies to be delivered by a Mid Husband, or in these egalitarian days, a Mid Person.

I can see him now, a large uncouth man with curly ginger hair, grimy hands and a lamp on his helmet.

I had a narrow escape when he blew up my nostrils, as he was smoking a pipe at the time. I had a birthmark on my shoulder where the hot ash fell.

I have forgiven him this but another disfigurement he perpetuated on my newborn person still embarrasses me so much that I always keep my pullover on when I go swimming. He tied a Granny Knot in my umbilical cord.

In the land of my birth April the First falls on Shrove Tuesday and besides wetting the baby's head with Newcastle Broon Ale, it is an imperishable custom to feed the newborn with a fresh made pancake which must be prepared by the mother.

It was whilst preparing this delectable dish that my mother inadvertently dropped me in the mixing bowl and I became the first battered baby in history.

My hopes of approaching manhood were given a great boost one day as I lay in my cot crowing and distinctly heard my mother say 'That's my little man'.

Peering over the side in all directions I realised we were alone and she was addressing me. I nodded my head in agreement and she immediately called me 'Her little baby'. WOMEN!! You can't believe a word they say.

'If this is childhood,' I said, 'Count me out' – and I grew up.

Christmas Day in The Workhouse

Towards the end of the First World War, when I was eight years old – the second youngest in a miner's family of six girls and three boys – we all dressed in our Sunday best, under our thickest, warmest clothes, on Christmas morning and climbed into a two horse waggonette, sent by the Guardians, to be driven off to the workhouse. Dad sat up on the box with Kit Peacock, the driver. Five of my sisters were grown up and the second eldest had our baby in her arms. I was tucked into my mother's voluminous skirts to keep the draught from my bare knees.

My oldest brother was away in the Navy. My other brother, the family black sheep, kept reciting a poem about what to do with Christmas pudding, which sounded silly to me as he never seemed to remember the last line – and my oldest sister looked daggers. My mother kept her eyes averted and I could see by the back of Dad's neck he was furious. Kit Peacock's shoulders kept shaking as though he was laughing.

I remember it was not really a very cold day for Christmas and when we crossed the waggonway and set off down the Fell, Kit put the horses into a trot towards the little town of Chester-le-Street, whose spire was a land-mark in our county of Durham. We had to wait at the level crossing until the coal-waggons passed for Blackfell pit was working full-time in the war effort.

There's nothing quite like the sound of trotting horses. In no time at all the whole family was singing. It began with carols but soon developed into a rehearsal of part songs, trios, quartets and solos, till at last I was made to say my recitations, which I did in a spiritless monotone to drive my eldest sister frantic.

'You'll have to put more expression into it than that,' she bawled.

'Now, now,' said Mam, pouring oil. He'll be alright when the time comes. He's got them off to a T.'

It took about two hours to reach the town and the older ones got out to walk up to the steep High Street. Kit drove his team through the arch into the Lambton Arms yards and we all walked the last short distance along Ropery Lane.

'Here we are,' said Dad as we came to a big iron gate set in a high brick wall. It was opened by an old man who addressed my Dad as 'Jim Lad' as they hugged each other.

We walked up a roadway towards a low red brick building, through an archway and into a grass courtyard surrounded by a square of mellow, red brick walls. A few hardy old chaps sat out on the sunny side on wooden benches. We waited while Dad shook hands with all of them. Some got out pieces of rag to wipe their eyes and noses. One old chap responded to a pat on the back with a prolonged bout of spitting and coughing.

Mr. and Mrs. Dunn the Workhouse Master and Matron welcomed us. He looked a stern little man but Mrs. Dunn was a real motherly body, beaming with bosom and backside all in black frills, with a sparkling white apron and cap. Soon we were having a cup of tea served by two pallid young ladies dressed, as were all the other females in long, rough, blue skirts and blouses.

We sat on wooden forms at a long table with a paper cloth. Dad and Mr. Dunn talked a lot about the Guardians. My sister, Lil, the family pianist went off with Mrs. Dunn and returned with a red face.

'That will be alright, Mrs. Dunn,' she said in her lying voice and then, in an aside to us, with a grimace, 'The piano's as flat as a pancake.'

'Let's get a start,' said Dad, 'We want to be onto the road again by two.'

We were taken to a big dining room, where perhaps sixty folks, old and young, sat on wooden benches at long tables set around the walls. Big bunches of holly hung from the gas lights and paper streamers crossed and re-crossed the room. The tables were covered with white paper and set with knife, fork and spoon at each place. All this I took in at a glance but what I was really looking for was the platform. To my horror there was none. A little chap needs a platform to recite.

We sat in a group around the piano. Mr. Dunn told the inmates how lucky they were to have a concert party to entertain them on Christmas Day and the show was on.

No platform, dead acoustics, a flat piano; I could see were weighing hard on my sisters as Dad stood up and told these old mining folks that he was a miner and honoured to bring his bairns to share their Christmas with them.

The air of expectancy was electric: the 'house' was alive; I could feel the warmth of it and guessed I would be 'thrown to the lions' after the opening chorus of:-

'Hail smiling morn
It tips the hills with corn.
Whose rosy fingers
Open the gates of heaven.'

My Dad lifted me up and stood me on a table and I held forth on the subject of 'Our Baby'. The air was full of joy. Old gaffers clapping their thighs, aglow with toothless laughter. The flatter the piano the tighter the harmony and the applause so warm the whole thing took wings.

Alec in a stage whisper gave instructions on plum pudding disposal. For once he managed his violin without snapping a string and my sister, Edie's, contralto, 'I Passed By Your Window' put lumps in all the throats. Everyone sang the carols. The finale, 'Keep the Home Fires Burning', was triumphant. You could feel it was a good concert.

The next item was more to my taste – Christmas dinner; and, would you believe it, Mr. and Mrs. Dunn and all our family, including me, served all the dinners. I was amazed at how these old folks were allowed to wolf their food. Many of them didn't waste time on the cutlery and the memory of toothless gaffers wrestling with the pork crackling was a standard topic with us for years to come.

Second helpings. As we all filed through the kitchen past the serving Mr. and Mrs. Dunn, we all said the same thing. 'No gravy, please. Just meat this time with no gravy.'

'Why, why?' I asked Alec.

'Wait till you see what they do with the Christmas pudding,' he said mysteriously.

The ride home was an anti-climax but my abiding memories of Christmas Day in the workhouse were being hugged by so many old folks who smelled like my grandfather, who kept a herd of goats; and of asking my Dad why it was called a workhouse, when they were all too old to work –

'Why did the old men sit out on a cold day?'
'Old miners have to keep spitting, son.'
'Why didn't they like the gravy, Dad?'
'Because they put the dinner in their pockets for after.'

The Ballad of Eighton Banks

(*Sung to the tune of Old King Coal*)

Now our street was a very fine street
As any one here will yield
Its name was Springfield Avenue
So we called it Pasture Field.
Now every man had a very fine house
And a very fine house had he.

LAST LINE OF VERSE.
'This bloody hoose is like hell' said the RANSONS.

CHORUS
Mick and Archie squealed.
There's none so rare as can compare
With the boys of Pasture Field.

Now Elders lad had a very strict Dad
And he never got very much fun
He couldn't get away with his pals to play
Till he had his homework done.
'Come and get your homework done' said the ELDERS.

Now Mr. Hooper had a very high wall
Of sandstone and cement.
And every time I kicked the ball
That's where the damned thing went.
'Who kicked the ball ower the waall?' said the HOOPERS.

John Thomas Smith lived next door up
He never said very much
'Cos he had a 'pediment in his speech
And Rabbits in his hutch.
'Hun, Hun, Hun, how's yer bun?' said SMITHY.

15

Now Adams had an Irish dog.
He took me for a bone.
I never bit that mongrel but
I was a bloody good shot with a stone.
'We's been clottin wor dog?' said the ADAMS.

Next come the Jeffersons, got no kids,
They didn't believe in play
And if you stopped outside their house.
You'd always hear them say,
'Get yersel away from here' said the JEFFERSONS.

Now Fifteen's where the Horsleys lived
They had a son called Jack
His mouth was big and open wide
And both his eyes were black.
'We's been hittin wor Jack?' said the HORSLEYS.

Now Teddy Pallister had a foot ball
And liked to pick his team.
You couldn't get a place if he didn't like your face
He only picked the cream.
'Nee body what says eh!' said the PALLISTERS.

Now old Ned Robinson used to keep
His Rabbits by the score
And every blade of grass was his.
Now touch it if you dor.
'Put that Rabbit meat doon' said the ROBINSONS.

Now twenty three was Ransons hoose
All full of dogs and kids
And what poor missus Ranson said
Is worse than what she did.
'This bloody hoose is like hell' said the RANSONS.

And later in that very hoose,
The Halls lived. Get this rhyme,
She was a well built lady who just
Kept abreast of the time.
'Breest like a geet football' said the HALLYS.

On Jimmy Haig, I'm rather vague,
Except his vegetable Diet
Our Alec called him 'Maneater'
And taught us kids to cry it.
'Wait till aa catch ye' said JIMMY.

Mick stood a tin on Marsden's wall,
Aa let bleeze with a waaller
I missed the can and off we ran,

It went right through their parlour.
'We hoyd the waaller in the parlour' said the MARSDENS.

Now 'Billy Brown's' has been pulled down
Yet has undying fame
For round the back was a stony track
With a most uncommon name.
'Up Billy Brown's backside' said the BRAYSONS.

Every year to Church we'd go,
Farewell to old Tom Bruce
Each sermon lasted till the next
Because his tongue was loose.
'And eh and eh and eh.' said BRUCY.

Now Jimmy Atkinson could preach
But boy he made me squirm,
For every bloomin' sentence
Was like a thrush with a damn great worm.
'Gunk, Gunk, Gunk.' said JIMMY.

At Ranters Chapel you will know
George Blakey was the despot
He came back from the war and prayed
'Goard bring pace to mespot'
'Pace to mespot bring.' said BLAKEY.

The Yeamon Family grew so big
They slept upon a line
And Arthur said 'Come in for some bread
Me Ma lost count at nine.'
'You're not one of wors' said the YEAMONS.

I once tapped big Mick's shin at football
Then he split my head.
I passed that way the very next day
His Gran rushed out and said,
'Don't you touch my Moike.' said the MELVINS.

The big deep gutter by Ramsey's house
Was the end of our race.
I came in last and jumped in fast
Right on Bill Ramsey's face
'Wee jumped on Bills face?' said the RAMSEYS.

Now Kitler's house was a colourful house
The garden never drab
Had rhubarb grown in chamber pots
And a damned great hansom cab.
'Come and have a ride on the cab.' said VINCY.

Now Johnson lived at No. I
His goose gog trees grew strong
He waited till they all grew ripe
But he waited just too long.
'We pinched my goose gogs?' said MATTY.

Now Elder's lad had a rickety bike
With two flat wheels and all.
To remind him to take his pump with him
He wrote it on Clegg's wall
'Who wrote "pump" on the wall?' said MANNY.

For wor Daisy's ower sixty club.
To the neighbours who put up with young Tommy Elder.
Hertfordshire 1972.

STONE WARS

The Village

Although our village of Eighton Banks was within earshot of collier boats on the river Tyne and had four pits within a mile of its centre it was not the usual huddle of red or yellow brick rows about a pit heap; it was built almost entirely of random sandstone and the hill of spoil at its centre was the remains of a long defunct sandstone quarrying industry.

Behind the sixty foot escarpment at the top of our street lay about 20 acres of broken stone hills and quarries from which the once famous Springwell Grindstones were exported world wide. The village was loosely scattered in three areas about the hill. To the east where once the Sandstone was cut by giant saws, lay the aptly named Sandy Lane area. to the south, were three well built stone avenues which never received their individual names, but were lumped together under the old name of the site – Pasture Field. The north end of the village petered out towards the tram terminus leading to the Tyne and its tough inhabitants derived their local name of the 'Ship Laners' from the depressed locality that lay about their notorious pub, 'The Ship.'

The village church school was towards one end of the village and took all the Sandy Laners and most of the Pastures Fielders. A new school had opened nearer the Tyne and a mile away but here was better equipment, classrooms and tuition; so to Harlow Green I went and here I lived, fought, played and grew up with the barefoot Ship Laners amongst whom I found stout friends and implacable enemies.

19

The Battle Ground

The sandstone hills were a boy's paradise, covered with rocks and stones
of every size; with deep ravines left by the quarries, some filled with eerie
green blue water on which our cissy parents forbade us to sail our home
made rafts of pit props. One quarry used to be frequented by a group of
deaf mutes who sought privacy for their rudimentary communications.
This place is still called the Dummie's Quarry, although it is now the
hideout for the village Pitch and Toss school with lookouts posted in the
gorse against police raids.

Heather and gorse were the only plant life and made magnificent fuel
for the Guy Fawkes Holocaust when whole acres blazed. The stones
made perfect building material for camps and we played soldiers on the
hills all the summer and winter long. The cinema had not yet inoculated
us with Cowboys and Indians. We never dreamt of the Ray Gun and
Laser Beam or even the pistol. We were Stone Age men and fought with
stones. Thousands of them of all shapes and sizes.

Many of our games were based on stones, such as Booling, Holey and
Duckstone and all tended to perfect the aim of the thrower. The bird life,
consisting of larks cheepers and jackdaws, led a very precarious existence
as they provided our only moving targets except for the odd rabbit and
the rats on the tip. Or did they? During my early childhood I had
witnessed several battles on the hill and had been dragged home by an
older brother when the Sandy Laners had pelted the Pasture Fielders
right back into the avenues. There they stood arrogantly on the cliff top
until the red face and blue uniform of our local bobby appeared along
the top road and whole armies evaporated to the cry of 'Pollis!! Pollis!!'

Skirmishing

The last battle I took part in was at the age of ten. During the first week
of the holidays Mick and Archie, Jack Horsley, Joe Humphrey, Bill
Ramsay and I built a magnificent camp on The Hill. Using really big

stones for foundations, the walls were able to support a roof of old bedsteads, heather, gorse and turf. To us, it was invisible except for a wisp of blue smoke from the corn beef tin chimney. We played there for several weeks and its popularity recruited at least twenty Pasture Fielders.

Going up the street one day I saw heavy smoke over the hill and thinking Horsley or Mick had set the roof on fire, tore up the track. The camp was a shambles of smouldering brush wood, but no Mick or Jack was about. They turned up later from the Sandy Lane direction shouting and swearing: 'The bloody Sandys done it.' Dixon and young Wilkie: We saw them run away and pelted them right into Thomas Street.' 'Did you catch them Mick'? 'No! but there's a broken window at Wilkie's'!! We sat about our smouldering ruin until big Bill Ramsey, Joe Humphrey and the others came up. 'This means war' said Bill with finality. The whole thing seemed to blow over and we rebuilt our camp at the bottom of a dell. More secluded but it proved a fatal mistake as soon as we were lulled into a false state of security and stopped posting look-outs.

We all looked up one day as a rumbling noise came from above and the roof began to sag. Scrambling out we were greeted by a roar from at least ten Sandys rolling big stones down the slope. 'Take cover!' yelled Bill Ramsey coolly and hunting frantically for stones we pelted back at the enemy from the shelter of the camp wall. The Sandys retaliated with a hail of rocks and despite our best efforts we realised the hopelessness of our plight, sitting ducks grouped closely below the enemy and no real ammunition. The Sandys seemed to see victory in sight and to yells of 'Charge! Charge!' they hurtled down upon us. 'Retreat! Retreat!' yelled Bill, and regardless of all cover we tore up the other side, grabbed stones, turned round and reversed the whole situation.

Spreading out we pounded the hapless enemy below who, now short of ammunition, filled the air with curses and threats of 'Wait till I get ye by yersell.' We now had the upper hand for no army charges uphill and when Jim Blacklock got hit in the leg and shouting 'Surrender!' started crawling back up the hill the Sandys broke and ran for it left and right.

'Cease fire' commanded Bill Ramsey. 'And listen, Horsley, if I catch ye peltin a wounded man again I'll belt yer lug!!'

Tactics and Strategy

As far as I can recall in all the Stone Wars very few men were hit. The worst casualty was a prisoner tied to a post on whom someone worked off an old school grudge with a stick. There was a lull for a few days but the whole village knew a storm was in the offing.

Our scouts brought rumours of the Sandys recruiting as far away as Black Fell. Our Pasture Field contingent of about twenty boys never went on The Hill less than ten strong and look outs were posted at once. Bill Ramsey was a real leader and really planned ahead. Where stones were scarce we hid stockpiles at strategic positions. We dismantled some barbed wire around Wally's field and laced it into the heather on our front. We would be out-numbered by the Sandys on a big turn out and aimed to retreat to our own choice of battle grounds.

If forced to fight on the run, start off with a cap full of stones. When the enemy advances retreat till he runs out of ammunition then turn and rout him. Always keep on high ground above your target. Such simple rules with a little discipline could outweigh bigger numbers. So said Bill and we believed him. Those were to be our tactics. To me Bill revealed his wider strategy. 'You're the only one who really knows The Shiplaners. We're going to need their help.'

The Ship Laners

The Ship Lane Gang went to the same school as myself. Their leader was Dobber Dobson a scrawny thirteen year old, with a cruel streak when roused, yet a gentle wistful chap when watching his pigeons. Potter Watson wore a brown jersey with what appeared to be leather cuffs through wiping his nose; Freddie Hare was always barefoot; Biggun Brayson, a little weed who had always gone with bigger chaps, an amazing footballer; Leslie White who had an impediment and said 'Quely' for twelve, his mother, Aggie, was a holy terror, feared by all and sundry; John Dotchin who could be seen taking off at a run for home at seven o'clock when his brute of a father blew the whistle at the back door; Hobbler and Williker Gibson, more pigeon men, Hobler had a hole between his front teeth and could spit on a fly at four paces, Geordie Waples who having worn glasses from an early age was unable to see his opponent in a fist fight so developed a wrestling technique, with a bear hug that could uproot an oak. Geordie's father had not come back from the war.

This was 1920 and practically all these families were destitute. The brilliant politicians had concluded our victorious peace in 1918 shouting 'Make Germany pay, Make Germany pay!' and Germany was paying reparations in German coal, which put our victorious returning miners totally on the scrap heap in this 'land fit for heroes'.

Yes, the Ship Laners were tough. They had to be, for life was a battle. Some kept pigeons and others preferred whippets to catch the odd rabbit for the pot on the fells. When their fathers had money, they spent it on drink or dreamed of riches at Pitch and Toss.

A roll call of this formidable gang must include the more than formidable May Simpson, a thirteen year old Amazon who wanted to be a boy. She wore an old red woollen hat through which the lice pushed dandruff from her dingy hair, a long black dress of her mother's, men's cast off boots, no underclothes to speak of and looked as though she had never washed for years. She was a successful if unorthodox fighter, kicking your shins till you bent down, then ripping her nails up your face. My bond and standing with the Ship Laners arose from an accumulation of many things: I took windfall apples to school in the autumn, I played football with them, I was the possessor of that rare and wondrous conveyance a bike, and their captain Dobber and I were pigeon men, exchanging eggs and chicks; but most of all, from having been thrashed at school with them for taking pot shots from the bridge, at the man who rode shotgun on the pit waggons.

The Prisoner

There was an air of foreboding over the whole village. War was imminent. It was Friday. School would reopen on Tuesday. It wouldn't come at the weekend so it must be today. There were further complications, today was pay day for those at work and the Pitch and Toss school would be in the Dummie's Quarry with lookouts posted keeping us away. My immediate problem was how to get out of our house. I had six sisters and only one was younger than myself. I had two brothers older than I but both were away at work. My sisters filled the house with rumours and my every move was met with 'And where do you think you're going?'

The most watchful of my prison guards was my older sister Jennie. She had played very ably the role of little mother as my parents reared our brood of nine, but now that I was a man of ten years and a village warrior at that, she was painfully unwilling to give up her authority. Jennie was a simple pious woman, chapel choir, Christian Endeavour, Girl's Friendly Society etc. but all this took on a grander flavour when she went to play tennis on the only court in the village, at the vicarage, and found out how much more respectable church people were than mere chapel goers. Our first inkling of Jennie's reaching for higher things was when she stopped saying 'Me Muther' and addressed our startled Matriarch as 'MOTHER' as in 'MOTH'.

The next concession to High Church was when I was dragooned into reciting at a Vicarage teaparty. To my horror I was introduced as Our Peter ('Tommy is such a common name' she whispered) to a typical collection of old and young fogeys. But the crowning shame was my presentation in white shorts and sailor blouse before a grinning company of boy scouts, with pocket knives swinging from their belts and badges up to their arm pits.

I will draw a veil over my embarrassing ordeal during the light entertainment. Jennie held forth á la Ella Wheeler Wilcox with her eyes reaching up into the rafters as if watching for the holy dove to descend. Next came refreshments, as a horse faced lady neighed, 'To be sarved by the Boy Scouts themselves.' The lads had been highly amused at my expense and I couldn't help thinking it was no accident when a hairy legged, pimply faced ape spilt half a cup of hot tea on my bare knee. By a strange coincidence the next chap to pass me with a tray tripped over my feet. The pandemonium which followed was, to say the least, beyond my expectations, for in no time at all I was half way home with Jennie hauling at my arm and holding forth about my ultimate fate.

'You'll never go to heaven.'

'Will all the church people go to heaven Jennie.?'

'I'm sure they will.'

'Then I want to go to hell.'

'Oh, you blaspheme as well do you? Just wait until I tell yer mutha.'
'You mean Mother don't you?' Jennie and I grew up in what is best
described as armed neutrality and now that I wanted to escape to the hills
I didn't make my move until she had gone off to catch the tram to
Newcastle. My favourite escape procedure when under observation was
to stroll out leaving the back door open, so that they could all see me
ambling nonchalantly up the garden whistling. My mother used to fall
for this, but my Dad was psychic. Once up the garden, I kept up the
whistling and circling back to the shed, mounted my byke and pedalled
swiftly past the back door.

My Dad was at the gate first. 'Your'e not gannin up the hills are ye
lad?'

'Not on me byke surely, Dad!'

'Why mind ye divent.' A painful pause ensued which he gallantly
broke with, a change of subject. 'I hear ye had two eggs from Jonna
Smith's best pair last week. I tell't ye nee mair pigeons here. What did ye
dee with them?'

'I gave 'em to Dobber Dobson Dad; he's been wantin that strain ever
since Jonna won. I don't want any more pigeons Dad. Ta Ra,' and I
pedalled slowly down the Pasture Field in the opposite direction to my
goal but still able to feel Dad's eyes in the small of my back. My byke was
a rare and ancient bone shaker handed down from an older brother. It
had drop handlebars; an uncommon sight in 1920 and I had turned them
upside down in the interests of stability, for the frame was too big for
me, necessitating even blocks on the pedals till my legs stretched.

I lowered the saddle by mounting it directly on the frame. This gave
me corns on my backside and a tendency to stand up on the pedals,
wobbling from side to side. Not a pretty sight I was told. My Dad used to
say I rode like my Mam walked: 'Bouncing off one foot onto the other'. I
could still feel his eyes on me as I neared the end of the road but forbore
to look back, for the last time I did so, I rode straight into the hedge, to
his unbridled amusement. Once out of sight, I accelerated along the bank
up the second avenue and back to the hill path. Shoving my byke in
Easton's yard I ran up the stony lane.

Pincer Movement

Not a soul was in sight. Near the peak I dropped on all fours, crawled between gorse bushes and peered out over the hills. It was a beautiful day. Heat haze shimmered over the screes, the gorse was ablaze with bloom and alive with bees; some distant shouting came from the Sandy Lane direction. A faint wisp of smoke showed near our camp but not where the chimney was.

I rose quietly and moved off towards it. Suddenly a black-bird shot out of a bush and fled chattering her alarm call. A figure rose behind a distant wall and made a forbidding sign. The gambler's look out. Before I reached the camp I came upon a figure sprawled on the track moaning. It was young Horsley. 'What the hell's happened to you?' 'I tripped over our barbed wire and Bill made me stay here. Ten of them have gone to take a look'.

'Let's have a look at your leg, you look terrible'. Jack showed me his wound. It was nothing. Then I saw the pipe and matches on the grass. 'Blimey Horsley you won't half get a howkin when Bill comes back. That poor pitman is going to be dying for his smoke when he comes back from work the neet. Put it back where you found it!!'

The wretched Jack could only groan 'Stay with me. Stay with me'.

'Not me. The Sandys must be out in force today and we'll need every man. I might even have to get the Ship Laners. How long have they been gone?'

Jack only groaned. 'Go and put that pipe where you found it. I'm off'. I broke into a trot for Sandy Lane. Our chaps must be up to their necks in trouble. As I topped each slope I crouched and took a look along the track. My caution paid off, for hurrying towards me came two boys and one of them was Nick Lewis. I was in no need of publicity and raced off to the right where I could take cover in the gorse on the lip of the escarpment. Here I lay greatly puzzled as to why they should enter our territory and, looking up to see if they had passed by, was dismayed to see them turn off towards my hiding place. There was nothing for it but to bolt over the brow and down a steep track which led to the main road. I was about to make a dash when voices broke out ahead and Jim Blacklock came into view scrambling over the edge leading a gang of Sandy Laners. I dived into a gorse bush and froze. What I heard as I lay there, over the pounding of my heart was easy to put together. Blacklock's gang were doing a pincer movement and Lewis having come through the hills knew the road was clear for them to take our lads from behind. By the time they were out of earshot I had made up my mind that I had to get to Sandy Lane before them. If they travelled with any sort of caution I had about 20 minutes to reach our patrol. Thank God for my old byke. I bounded down the hill into the main road and tore back to Easton's yard. Tommy Elliot was riding my bike around as I burst through the gate. He jumped off red faced. 'Just having a try.' he stammered.

'That's alright Tommy. Listen! We've got work to do. The hills will be swarming with Sandys in half an hour.' Tommy got the idea and ran off towards the Pasture Field to recruit help while I pedalled off in the opposite direction.

Retreat

I dumped my byke in Arnold's the Builder's yard, climbed the fence and shot into the hills. I could hear the sounds of battle now as I reached the top and the odd stone came overhead. The sight was amazing. A hundred feet below was Sandy Lane, full of boys and just below me on a lower slope of the scree was our gang literally in their back yard with all the stones they needed, a vertical throw and their tails well up. The row was fantastic. The Sandys had to offer themselves as targets to get ammunition and I saw Joe Humphrey just roll a waller over the edge where it leapt and bounded down into the street followed by an avalanche of smaller stones which the Sandys immediately picked up and threw back with yells of rage. Not many shots reached us but following back to the source of one I glimpsed the figure of Big Lenny Wilkinson shaking his fists. He was sixteen. The veterans were being called out. This was going to be some battle.

Bill Ramsey started on to me for being late, but soon tumbled to the Sandy's strategy and stopped the action. We withdrew on the run and were soon throwing ourselves over the fence into the builder's yard. We were not a minute too soon. We could hear the Sandys baying up the hill in anticipation of their pincer movement. The encircling patrol under Jim Blacklock appeared momentarily above us as they closed in for the kill. 'NOW' said Bill Ramsey 'RUN like hell. We'll make a stand on the home pitch!' As we clambered over the gate he shouted 'What you hanging about for?'

'Catch me byke, Bill'.

His eyes lit up 'Blimey just the thing. You take the road for it and try to fetch the Ship Laners. If Tommy Elliot brings the rest, we'll be holding the home ground. Good luck'. He was gone, loping along the hill track, turning to wave a derisive hand at the rising roar from Sandy Lane, urging the retreat, but still a wise leader, bringing up the rear and shouting 'Fill yer caps. Fill yer caps as ye gan!!'

The Amazon

As I turned into the main road and made off on my mission I was conscious of the magnitude of today's events. Here was war indeed and so far all I had done was ride my byke. My family would never believe it! Coming along the road were Sandy Lane citizens, from the Newcastle tram, carrying their shopping, nodding to me, answering my 'Good afternoon, Mrs. Gault. Good afternoon, Mrs Swan' quite unconscious of the turmoil that had hit their neighbourhood in their absence. It was seeing them, that made me realise as I neared Pasture Field, that it was odds on our Jennie would be on her way home. This was an encounter I just had to miss so I pulled in behind the Co-op butcher cart which turned into the road ahead of me and took off at a brisk trot. The butcher man was Jack Horsley's father. He would have been home for dinner, late from a pub, and would be making up for lost time.

My mother used to say his beery breath spoilt the meat. I could see the spring scales, joints of meat and links of sausage swinging wildly on their hooks, through the open back of the cart. He was driving so fast he sometimes left behind the cloud of flies that accompanied him on his round and I had to pedal through them. It was during one of these spurts that the cart stopped abruptly and having no choice I swerved past and ran smack into Mr Horsley as he stepped down from his driving perch. I refrain from recalling his first exclamation but I knew the meaning of all his swear words and with visions of a parental enquiry into the incident I apologised profusely. 'Oh it's thoo is it?' he said, abashed possibly at the thought of my retelling the whole story. 'I thowt thee would be up the hill. UWER Jack hasn't been home for his dinner.'

His south Durham dialect grated on my ears. A Geordie would say 'ye', not 'thou' and 'Wor Jack' not 'UWER'.

'EE man, Mr Horsley, aa diven't knaa where he is, am just gannin a ride on me byke. Sorry aa run inta ye.'

'If ye see 'im send him yem, Tommy.'

A knot of people had gathered. I took off. Our Jennie could be coming off the next tram, and already as I approached Ship Lane I could hear the triple rumble as it crossed over the waggon way. You couldn't just ride into Ship Lane casually. It was not just any old lane, it was a disaster area. I stood reconnoitring, hoping the natives would be friendly, with one eye on the street when a familiar figure came out of the Co-op and stopped to speak to her companion. I gasped. It was our Jen!! I dived into Ship Lane and was taking the first turning off when two dirty hands seized my handlebars and a voice said 'Let's have a ride Tommy;' I looked up into the smoky eyes of May Simpson. This was disaster. Talk about the devil and the deep blue sea. If our Jennie just saw me in Shiplane that would be the end of my career for all time, but if she saw me in Ship Lane talking to May Simpson I would be beyond redemption.

I had to get rid of May. 'You can have a ride May.' I said urgently 'but tell me where is Dobber Dobson?'

'He'll be up the allotments at his pigeons.'

'You ride up and tell Dobber I want to see him and all the lads. He'll know what I mean.'

'I can't go' said May, 'I dasent leave here. Me Father's look out over the quarry to day and I gotter watch and tell him if the copper comes off the tram'. I knew May's drunken father, Dick Simpson. He was too slow to play Pitch and Toss but earned a little beer money as a look out and here he was, apprenticing May to the trade. I could feel our Jennie prattling around the corner and had a brainwave. 'You go and fetch Dobber, May and I'll stop here and watch for the Pollis.'

'Promise', said May.

'Blimey you're taking my byke aren't you? I won't go far. I must see Dobber now.'

'I'll go' said May hoisting her raggy skirt and throwing a dirty leg over the crossbar, making me wonder how she'd cope with that iron saddle.

'Don't sit on the seat!' I shouted. May turned shakily in a circle and came back ominously towards me, yelling 'If you think you're bloody saddle is too good for my .... 'No, No, I didn't mean that,' I cut her invective off. 'It's a dammed hard saddle and it hurts.'

As she wobbled away up Capston Lane I rushed to the corner and peeped out. Jennie was just finishing her conversation. Calling down blessings on heaven I dived into the alley. Seconds later Jennie minced primly into view, glanced up at the receding figure of May, did a double take and watched her out of sight. Not till then did she proceed, shaking her head as she went. My heart was asking had she seen only the disgusting sight of a girl trying to ride a man's byke or did she know the whole truth? Time alone would tell and fate would decree that when I came to guess I would guess wrongly. In no time at all May came back followed at a leisurely pace by the lanky figure of Dobber and the two Gibsons. 'The copper hasn't come off the tram May' I volunteered as she executed a highly spectacular dismount with her skirts caught on the saddle. 'The copper isn't in town Tom, Dobber has been watching him floating about at the other end of the allotments. We think he's waiting for the men to come back that way from the quarry.'

'I guess that's what he's up to' said Hobler Gibson, 'you'll have to skip off and tell your Dad, May, before they walk into the trap'. Dobber was watching me closely.

'What's the score Tom?'

'Dob; the Sandys are on the warpath cos Bill Ramsey took a patrol into their backyard. When I left, the boys were in full retreat back to our end but they'll be heavily outnumbered. There looked to be thousands of Sandys'.

'How many men has Bill got?'

'About ten when I left but Tommy Elliot was combing the avenues for the rest'.

'We need all the help you can give us Dobber'.

'That's O.K. Tom, we owe the Sandys a showdown and we've been looking forward to it'.

'Where's the rest of the gang?'

'There's a football game on the tip,' piped up May.

'Lets go' said Dobber taking charge. As we ran towards the top. May trundled along behind on the byke. All but a few of the players grabbed the bits of clothing that had marked the goal posts and joined us. A battle was a much more exciting prospect than football. There must have been twenty of us all together, all talking at once.

'Shut up' said Dobber, 'and listen'.

'The Sandys will be above Pasture Field now. We can't go through the middle track cos the Pollis is in the allotments. We'll have to go around Galloping Green and in by the Quarry, to come up behind them'.

'You can't go through the quarry', said Geordie Waples, 'If the gamblers are there'.

Here May who had been showing off her skill on my byke broke in.

'My dad'll clear the quarry when I tell him where the copper is'.

'Follow me and not so much noise', Dobber loped away ahead. The army fell in at the double, May brought up the rear on the byke. From Galloping Green to Favell's Gates we ran on the railway line; then through the plantation into the deserted Pit Pony Field. Dobber quieted the gang and ushered them all into an empty stable. 'Quiet! Stop here till I come back!'

Dobber, May and I ran along behind a wall towards the quarry lip. Suddenly a head appeared above the wall.

'What's going on? What you doing here lass? I tell't ye te watch the trams!'

'Father, the Pollis is laying in wait in the allotments'.

'Is that reet?' he glanced at Dobber.

'I watched him for an hour from my loft' volunteered Dobber.

'He's up to something fishy'.

'Ye done well May, Wait'.

Old Simpson climbed on the wall, put two fingers in this mouth, let out a piercing whistle then raised both arms above his head. After a while he got down on the other side.

'Thanks', he said. 'Ye'd best gan back the way ye came. I'll be off'.

He slithered out of sight.

'What now?' said Dob.

'Let them get clear of the quarry and we'll go through and come up behind the Sandys'.

'I'm coming with you' said May.

'You're not, May'! I butted in 'You're our dispatch rider. Go back to the stables; send the lads on here then ride back to Pasture Field. Get word to Bill Ramsey, we're on the way, and leave my byke in the corner of the Well Field by the stile'. May swelled with importance and hurried off.

Victory

Dobber and I climbed up and peered into the pit. It was deserted.
'What now?' said Potter Watson as the boys came up.
'Listen' said Dobber. 'We're going through the quarry and out to the top of hill path'.
'Can't we go through the fields behind the walls?' said Whitney who had a horror of cliffs.
'Not bloody likely!' said Dobber.
'They'll never dream we'll come through this way today'.
'Let's go and no more talking'.
'Let's get a move on,' I urged, 'or the war will be over before we get there'.
Once off the quarry floor and climbing the steep slopes towards the hill we could hear the faint shouts of the antagonists.
Dobber drew us off to the left towards a stony scree.
'It's easier that way', said Fred Hare, pointing right.
'Shut up and fill yer caps. Look sharp about it.'
Fully armed we crept on upwards and the nearer we came to the top, the louder came the sounds of battle.
'Stay here and keep quiet'.
Dobber and I wormed up on to the brow into the gorse, lay down and listened. A stone thumped into the gorse behind us and another. Somebody yelled, 'Look out your end! They're coming up behind the wall. Up here! Up here!' We peered out and down the scree. The Sandys were stood back from our battle ground too wise to leave good ammunition and charge up the slope. It was long range stuff with our blokes in good numbers strung out on the far slope and everybody yelling 'Charge!'
Big Wilkie was moving up away on the right with a group running towards the wall where our chaps were trying to outflank them.
'Look at that! Look at that!' said Dobber 'He's left the centre empty! Call them up and we'll split them wide open'. Pockets bulging, Caps full, the Ship Lane Gang looked a fearsome sight. Above the clamour over the gorse Dobber yelled, 'Stay in the middle on the stones. Don't follow anybody but me. Charge! Charge!' we dashed through the gorse into the breach and everything happened at once. Our yell brought a fantastic cheer from the opposite slope and the flying stones came like flocks of starlings.

The Sandys turned on us from two sides. 'Take them Tom. I'll go for Wilkie'. Wilkies' party up at the wall turned in dismay and as they did so Joe Humphrey's men stood up in the field behind them and let fly a barrage at close range. Dobbers' men halted and stayed with the ammunition. Wilkie was throwing his arm about and swearing. My hands were full on my side, a stone went over my shoulder too close for comfort and I started to look after myself. Geordie Waples, blood streaming from his face, was banging his opponent's head on the ground. Freddie Hare and Potter Watson, a close knit pair, stood on a small bluff together doing long range stuff on the left wing of the Sandys, now making a fighting withdrawal trying to look two ways at once.

'Fill yer caps! Fill yer caps!' shouted Dobber, already scenting the retreat, but retreat was not in Wilkies' mind. The big leader was not one to lose his head. As soon as Joe Humphrey's little band ran out of stones, Wilkies' men ran through them and away across the field, passing out of sight.

Bill Ramsey's charging army now advancing down the slope. Their heartening roar was the last straw for the Sandys, whose spirit collapsed at the sight of their fleeing leader. They broke in all directions breaking off and fleeing as the pugnacious Ship Laners showered rocks and taunts on their heads.

It was a rout.

'Let 'em go! Let 'em go!' shouted Bill Ramsey coming up to our stand. 'Good old Dobber' he said slapping him on the back. 'Let em go. We've had enough today.'

'Shall we chase Wilkie?' said Joe Humphrey. 'He must be making for the allotments.'

'Don't bother' said Dob. 'They'll run straight into the arms of the Pollis.'

'Gor Blimey' yelled Bill, slinging his hat full of rocks in the air: 'What an end for Wilkie. Clear the hill before the balloon goes up'.

Nemesis

That evening it was a triumphant little band of Pasture Fielder's that gathered in the deep ditch in the Well Field. I hadn't been home for tea for I knew I'd never get out again. Mick brought me some bread and dripping when he came out. I'd lit a little fire of twigs in the ditch. Bill Ramsey and Joe Humphrey and several of the others came later and we all sat and bragged about our doughty deeds of the afternoon.

'Did you see Geordie Waple's face streaming with blood?'

'That's nowt, did you see Blacklock when Geordie was finished with him?'

'Jack Horsley's bad in bed. The Sandys knocked him about when they took him prisoner'.

'That's not right! Jack was sick as a dog when they caught him. He'd been smoking twist'.

'Is that right Wilkie's lot ran straight into the Pollis?' 'We'd have been swamped if the Ship Laners hadn't turned up'. 'You should have seen the Sandys faces when you came out of the whins'. It went on and on and on. We couldn't leave it alone.

Each man relived his feats; it got later and later, we threw sticks on the fire, the flames rose and with them our voices rang across the meadow.

We never heard him come until he was standing above the ditch. Our Pollis McCaffey, the flash of his buttons exploded us in all directions. The Ransons made straight for home, the others ran around and towards the top road. My house was at the other end of the street, I was cut off. I crawled through the hedge and shot away out towards the farms through the tall grass.

After the first panic stricken burst, I stopped and lay down to regain my breath and listen.

There was no sound of pursuit. A few doors banged in the avenue.

The dogs quieted down and I looked up at a beautiful sky full of stars. I resolved to go right around the hay field, join the Long Bank at Peacock's Lane and reach home from the opposite direction.

Before I climbed over the wall into the lane I listened, but the village seemed still. Here goes. My footsteps on the road sounded like drums after the quiet swish of the hay field. The prospect of home and the confrontation of my family loomed ominously nearer. I began to whistle for company. A figure was coming along the road in the opposite direction. I maintained my whistling until we were near enough for me to say 'Goodnight'.

'Goodnight' came back, an unmistakeable voice, the moonlight flashed on the Pollis' buttons. The temptation to run was terrible. My feet had that nightmare feeling of being glued to the ground but nothing happened and I maintained the same pace.

As we got farther apart, I wanted to resume whistling but forebore, for my expert whistling is as good as a trade mark. At the bottom of our road under the gas lamp I paused and listened. The steady tread continued unchecked in the distance. I allowed myself the luxury of thinking I'd outwitted old McCaffey. What a story it would make for the boys tomorrow.

'Tomorrow.' I said 'Tomorrow. You won't see any boys tomorrow or the next day or the day after that.'

A deep feeling of foreboding came over me as I went through my usual ritual before going into our house.

I dusted my boots off with my cap, stuffed my hair under it, pulled up my stockings, took a good sniff, then wiped my nose on my sleeve.

My whistling as I reached the door was to say the least, off key, and stopped abruptly at the sight of my assembled family, with the excited younger girls whispering; 'Here he is' as they eagerly awaited the execution.

My father laid aside his pipe and paper and looked at me over his specs. The youngsters looked at me giggling. My mother glanced once at me pitifully then kept her head down on her knitting. My sister Jennie stood up holding her needlework bundled in front of her looking coldly at me with eyes aglitter as though she had a hand grenade under her pinny.

'What time yer call this lad?'

'Sorry Dad'.

'You never came home for tea', cut in Jennie.

'Didn't feel like any Jen'.

'You won't get any supper', piped up Nancy.

'Be quiet' said Dad. 'What hev ye got to say for yourself?'

'Nothing, Dad'.

'Have ye put your byke away?'

'My byke.' I thought. 'Blimey where the hell was my byke?'

In confusion I rushed out stammering 'I'll see if it's in the shed, Dad'.

I returned sheepishly, stood where I had stood before.

'It's in the shed Dad'.

Then came the 1000 dollar question.

'Who do you think brought it home?'

'Don't know Dad'.

Jennie's eyes glittered. The kids were bursting to butt in.

'Who do you think brought it?' My mother looked up at me with pity and love, her eyes as always pleading for the truth at all costs.

I swallowed. 'Was it May Simpson?'

Though I knew I had dropped a bomb only the silence roared.

The kids put their hands over their mouths; Dad's specs fell off his nose, my mother started to knit.

Jennie's leer was uncanny to be hold.

'MAY SIMPSON' she intoned with deliberation, savouring each syllable and stepping back as from a leper.

Dad continued.

'What makes you think that, lad?'

'I loaned it to her this afternoon to go a message'.

The kids couldn't hold out any longer.

They burst out together.

'It was the Pollis'.

'The Pollis said ye left it in the field when ye ran away.'

'What de ye say to that?' came from Dad.

'You wicked, wicked, boy' piped up Jennie, triumphantly.

'Sorry, Dad'.

'Upstairs ye go. I'll be up'.

Once on the stairs, away from the heat of all those accusing eyes, I felt better. It was all over except for the hiding. I undressed for bed, feeling my buttocks in anticipation.

What did they always say. 'This is going to hurt me more than it does you'.

Well, they could be right.

I had corns on my backside already.

The 'Kitler' Saga

Pit Village Life 1900–1920

Should you chance to reach our village by the bottom road to town
And you're greeted by a figure that looks out and also down,
By a cheery flung enquiry as to if your 'Mackin' Back?'
Answer 'Yiss' and fall in with him, for you'll find him 'canny crack.'

Remark not on his crooked gait, stiff leg and wide flung stick,
He's not the first from 'Betty' Pit that's had to learn that trick.
His son did, my Grandpa, my Uncle, any fool knows miners' bones are
   cheap.
That's why they walk like three legged stools.

His face may be a wee bit coaly and his beard a wee unkempt
From the fastidious ablutions he is more or less exempt.
His shaggy mane that tails the wind supports a dut that may be brown
Its sombre hue is relieved where his hair peeps through the crown.

Could this venerable headpiece tell the tale of all its grime,
T'would involve a pageant, starting long ago before my time.
Fifty years at least have gone since first it crowned his thatch,
It's part of him that he will wear in heaven with wings to match.

Should this figure from the story book upraise your foolish pride,
And you answer not his cheery hail and pass the other side,
Keep on respectability, keep on, that judge men by their claes,
A man's a man for aa that, his wee world's a better place.

Laugh if ye wish, yon ancient head has borne the full load of this world of
   care,
Grim poverty and want have stalked his footsteps
Grief an sorrow greyed yon hair.

He has lived a life of labour 'cording to his highest lights,
He has known the pinch of hunger, fought with pain the sleepless night.
His story is a sacrifice to raise his young'uns right,
But there's no rest for poor folk, only death will stop his fight.

He has raised a tribe (forget their type),
His all has gone to keep a race.
However low his aim to yours it was his highest,
And he's won his place.

Man's duty is to be a man and hand the torch of human kind,
He's done his share right well, though men have laughed at him behind.
See him, ye modern age whose pleasured ease forbids a youngster's cry,
As one who took his burden up and grudged not his load e'en though he
    die.

Tho' he may sleep in yon old bowler, he doffs it weekly at the village Kirk,
And draws some kind of hope and strength that sees him safely through his
    week of work.
And when he quits this weary struggle, comes his time for mackin' back,
Peter's gate will open wide and Peter whisper 'Good old Jack!'

There's a side to that man's history, Unadulterated mirth
That's common knowledge, here it is: but first!! *ADMIT HIS WORTH.*
How strangely humour, pathos, romance, in his tale does blend,
I write it *kindly* as a privilege as a man writes of a friend.

Jack's family tree was but a stunted twig of village love.
His worthy sire, so it seems, was quite a hardy cove,
Whose airy fastness braved a height a thousand feet or more
Like eagle's eyrie on that frozen hill known as Tow Law.

His father kept some cows, they say, he also had a pump,
His street was Milk and Water Raa, he must have had a pump.
His address, Thomas Littlefair, of 14 Milk and Water Raa,
His chateau was Dan's Castle, and his home town was Tow Law.

This much is known of Jack before he came to our street,
And here we find him with a comely wife and house complete,
The lady's history's unknown but that is her affair,
We only take the story up where she is 'Littlefair.'

Whence came this name's a question which strangers often ask us,
Some think that it's a pun upon Jack's oversize proboscis,
For that is not a little affair, rude boys are heard to shout.
There's been a Hebrew up that family tree of his I doubt.

Our Joe still swears he saw Jack save his life with that great snout.
He slid right down a roof one-day but caught up on the spout.
The years have flown but time has made Jack's nose not one jot littler,
Although his name's got worn by use until it's now just 'KITLER'.

Jack's noble pile with h. and c. and all mod. con., large garden,
Is situate in its own grounds but stay, 'I beg your pardon!'
Not garden, for folks did remark to Jack's great consternation,
The increase of Jack's children meant a decreased vegetation.

The last lone flower in 1910 within yon bedstead pale
Was eaten by Kitler's wooden legged duck, and thereby hangs a tale.
This venerable fowl by some mischance had broken off a leg
And Jack replaced it dexterously by clipping a clothes peg.

Now Jack was quite a livestock man, cats, dogs and all the rest
And the tale of the death of Kitler's dog is really one of the best,
This canine marvel was a wild and woolly beast of prey,
And how it quit this mortal strife is more than I can say.

In hunger once it ate its tail, least so my father said,
And then it ate its body till at last it ate its head.
This theory is discredited by folks who say they saw
The fur of noble canus in a coat that Jack's wife wore.

However it went and not one word
From Jack could mortal wheedle,
He has now a whippet called Carmel
That can jump straight through a needle.

The tragic end of Carlo has a parallel far worse
In the shameful fate that overtook Kitler's old white horse.
This episode took place a year or two before my time,
This stuff is village legend but it must have been quite prime.

Jack's lady love to Jack's dismay, though I wish her no harm,
Developed a most prodigious thirst and liked to raise her arm,
And often down the High Street when my tram a pub did pass,
I've seen her gazing roofwards through the bottom of a glass.

The exploits of the lady bowed our hero down with shame,
So he withheld the finance to deter the little game.
But Bacchus will not be forsworn and thirst is quite a job,
One night she went and pawned Jacks's horse,
It raised but fifteen bob.

In Gateshead toon she quenched her thirst and bought some sausage meat,
A tidy bit of business, 'cause she liked to have things 'neat','
The 'neat' bit seemed to produce a mild intoxication,
At least her steering coming back was by approximation.

In pasture field the road was bad and hampered by her fuddle,
My lady stood on nothing and then lay down in a puddle.
And as she lay and pondered, maybe on the curse of drinks,
Old Melvin's dog on sausage fed and made some missing links.

Jack missed his horse and he waxed wrath, but being a drawing room
    writer,
I am constrained to record that he called his wife a 'blighter'.
To get the lurid details just ask anybody's marrow
Of how Jack brought her home in state and also, in a barrow.

As to the sequel of this tale history is mute,
Jack must have written off his capital, one horse to boot.
I cannot trace a link from here to what I've pondered hard,
A vehicle that stood for years in Littlefair's back yard.

Just athwart the garden pathway there it stood, an ancient cab,
I've played there with Jack's grandson, Vince, and often we would grab
Imaginary reins and ride on roads that fancy chose,
And Vincy used to think fine roads, though what with goodness knows.

He said a queen that carriage used and looking back I see her,
And thinking of the cab I'm sure it was Queen Boadicea.
Strange incongruities are real as life when you're a boy,
And even yet that cab recalls the Wooden horse of Troy.

That cab became a greenhouse and its precincts were forbidden,
When glass became a thing of the past they used it for a midden.
A laddie's mind can conquer ought and often I did stab
The driver, rob the bags of mail and flee on Kitler's cab.

Vince was my pal when we were kids and much time have I spent,
Upon the Littlefair estate on boyish pleasure bent.
I loved the happy-go-lucky folks and the daily domestic strife,
I accepted as the essence of real Bohemian life.

Vince was a grandson of the hero of this little tale
His home was packed with relatives of every social scale,
He told me all the dads and mams that made that Tower of Babel,
But I could never understand that genealogical table.

Now Vincy's pop, he left the war at home and went to France,
And came not back unfortunately or otherwise perchance,
Suffice to say that Vincy's Ma obtained the open air,
He may have been a sailor now, for sailors just don't care.

The widow soon a new mate found, a Belgian, some say Russian,
And some said things I fear are quite irrelevant to this discussion.
Vince used to weave a saga round this man from o'er the sea,
And often he would tell his wondrous parents' tale to me.

He called him by the grandest names and gave him princely manners,
His mother also called him names not seen on Chapel banners,
Many strange and lurid words I cherished to use later,
When Vincy cheated me at quoits I addressed him à la mater.

These nommes-de-plume, he once retold his ma, (a dirty trick)
The manner of her coming made me beat it double quick.
I often wondered why her name came to be Mary Ellen,
But as I ran from Kitler's yard I knew 'twas Mary Yellin.

The Russian prince has gone,
Perhaps his people crowned him,
I mind one day his wife tried to,
The pan was full, it drowned him.

Another sprang into the breach a widow's heart to let,
He must be tougher than the rest because he's still there yet.
He rules the roost no doubt of that but now there is no tellin',
It may be just the power of love but I oft' hear Mary Yellin.

This chappy Bob was even tough enough to set the garden,
And after years of football even concrete tends to harden.
He told me he set fifty spuds all in one straight line,
The hens ate one but still he bragged a crop of forty nine.

And once he set some rhubarb but it never made the pace,
I thought the things he used to force were rather out of place.
The innocent young rhubarb shoot that first peeped from a crack,
Shouted, 'Boys, we've grown to China and the rhubarb plants turned
    back!'

He tried his hand at runner beans but they just ran to skin,
And once he owned a greenhouse but the owner ran him in,
'I plant' said he 'but things won't grow: it sets me off the deep.'
Now he plants his feet on the mantlepiece and sets him off to sleep.

Another standard of the house is Kit, I'm not a mocker,
He is a lifelong compen case, but you should watch his soccer,
'Cause what Kit knows about compen is certainly worth knowing,
He's fleet of foot as any man but Doctor's day's bad going.

Kit was the family artist and music was his fort,
So much so that in days of yore he an old organ bought.
The neighbours within earshot used to hail its trumpet sound,
With claims that Kit and his organ were accoustically unsound.

It is my firm belief the Lost Chord was his favourite note,
I've often wished to find the chord and tie it round his throat.
Many's the time that folk have wished Kit's organ was in Hell,
And how it last went up in flames is what I'm going to tell.

Disaster came to Babel swift one early Winter's morn,
The ancient lodge went up in flames and all that 'Warn't in pawn'
Was lost to them in Holocaust ablaze from roof to floor,
The smoke poured through the window and the folks poured out the door.

'My organ! Save my organ!' Kit rushed into the blaze,
And Bob rushed in to help him, the crowd just stood amazed.
'Tis lost! 'Tis lost! my organ's fast.' The crowd all gave a cheer,
As Kit's voice pierced the smoke, 'My organ's fast on top of the steer'.

This seemed to check the salvage corps when Chrissy jammed the stair,
And from the upstairs window flew a flock of earthenware.
The crowd all cheered as slowly like some great ghostly kite,
A pair of outsize stays came floating down out of the night.

A blow like this one often finds leaves many broken hearted,
But soon as everything was cool, Jack got a trowel and started.
That noble soul stood up to fate when stronger men would wilt,
And this is chapter one, the tale, 'The house that old Jack built.'

About this time a building scheme nearby was operating,
The watchman was Matt Johnson and a sleuth of no mean rating.
The soul of honour I've no doubt, but horribly convenient,
He was Jack's brother in-law, you see, and may have been well lenient.

For Bobby married Kipper don't you know, and this relation,
Is credited by many with Jack's building operations.
Suffice to say, folks tell that Jack did take his barrow and borrow,
Material from the builder intending to ask tomorrow.
Firm being his conviction that tomorrow never comes,
And firmer his conviction Brother Matty never comes.

Like Phoenix from its ashes rose the house of Littlefair,
The upstairs rooms were occupied before Jack built the stair.
And 'ere the chimney pot was fixed, the last slate put in place,
The tribe was back and Donnely's Lodge would take a poor third place.

For all Jack's sons had wives and bairns, his daughters bairns and men,
Their numbers overran his house, their names outran his ken.
'Tis said they slept upon a rope and managed rather fine.
They say the reveiller's hectic when Grandpa cuts the line.

One noble son a cobbler is and plies right well his trade,
He's good at vulgar repartee, his name for spade is spade
With blood on and his foes oft' leave him going fast,
My pal once paid him a dud bob and ducked to dodge the last.

The cobbler's name's Mac-Henry, the village waits to see,
When Jack will assent his authority and try Mac-Henry flee.
For there's much domestic humour and a wee domestic strife
The table talk I fear would oft defy the cobbler's knife.

Jack's dropped the building business except for a door pergola,
Which, fell upon Mac-Henry's head, the last made a dent in Jack's bowler.
And so the tale goes on till all Jack's bairns are fully grown
But once they've become adults they have started on their own,
And Ivy Cottage still persists to provide a situation
For warring grown ups and a playing younger generation.

This saga wouldn't be complete without a little verse,
On Vincy as a cyclist. Now Vince gets verse and verse,

Somewhere he got some old byke wheels, translate, 'GOT' with freedom.
I know he got'em somewhere, Micky Melvin said he, 'seed'im'.

He only wanted just a frame and chanced to ask my father.
'An old byke frame' said Pop. 'We have. It's yours now look no farther.
And if there's anything ye want just come and get it nuw.'
And Vincy came and got it. How it got Vince I'll shew.

The great day dawned: the complete iron steed stood in the yard,
And part of Vincy's pants were there, the paint was hardly hard.
He rushed around and told his pals, he'd show 'em how to ride,
'Now boys, come round tomorrow' said he, 'when the paint gets propl'y
    dried.'

But meanwhile Vincy's sisters, interfering women like,
Thought it would serve a dual purpose as a lady's byke.
They got an ancient hacksaw and then to Vincy's shame,
They seized his mangle unawares and cut out half the frame.

Quoth Vincy to his pals next day, 'Now boys, behold! I cycle.'
'It looks a bit shaky to me,' said one, a Melvin and a Michael.
But Vincy, pedalling down the street, just turned his handles south,
When up they came and hit him such a wallop in the mouth.

The mangle folded up and Vincy loosed a deafening holla,
The mudgard was a necktie and the front wheel was a collar,
The road was strewn with bits of Vince and balls and little rollers,
When Vincy coughed he shot big Mick with several of his molars.

Then up he got on to his feet and called his sisters names,
I wrote them on some paper but it burst out into flames.
So ends a cycling career and still Vince does not like,
To hear you say on passing,
'Now Vince, how's your byke?'

Now Vincy's grown up to a man of whom we folks are proud,
He is a budding athlete, idol of the soccer crowd.
His past has given him a keener sense of values which,
Is not vouchsafed to folks whose parents are a trifle rich.

He'll face the world much better than a son of luxury's lap,
He's got a keeness in his eye from poverty's handicap.
These are our folks, the salt of earth, the heroes left unsung,
Born in squalor, reared on pittance from hard labour rung.

Their fathers slaved and toiled in ignorance's night,
But these younger folk are witnessing the growth of learnings light.
Those who have seen and felt the pinch of poverty's grim blight
Are slowly realising what's their simple human right.

As wisdom's sun is dawning, life's indomitable trend
Says the courage of our poor folk will attain it in the end.
And so come back to old Jack, he may know not what he is,
But I'd like to think I'll serve my folks as well as he's served his.

He's given time and strength and life itself his people for,
Is there a nobler gesture? Could mortal man do more?
And mackin' back to Peter's gate, he'll shout 'Pete, are yer in?'
And Pete will shout, 'Wey Aye Jack. Take yer dut off, howay in'.

Eighton Banks 1926

USWORTH versus the Rest

Eighton Banks 1933

In the season 1923-33 Usworth mixed Hockey team not only topped the Tyneside mixed Hockey League but beat the rest.

Oh list all ye who wish to hear our noble Usworth's praise,
I tell of the thrice famous match she won in ancient days,
When we were strong and won the league in no uncertain manner,
Hail Usworth mightier than the rest. The cup's on Walton's pianner.

Our skipper was a mighty man who helped to win the ashes.
His loins were gird in thermogene, he twirled his black moustaches
And cried to Beetham loud and long, 'We've won the league you see:
We'll play the whole of the blinking rest and beat them all' said he.

Then Beetham like a beet went he, his face grew red and dark.
'I take your challenge. Tomorrow' said he. 'We'll come to Usworth Park.
Ten teams you'll play all at a blow. T'will stop your blooming chatter.'
'Bring twenty teams' said Watson; 'To us it makes no matter.'

The field was set, a sight to see the Usworth's stalwart eleven.
The pitch was hard and not a cloud appeared to mar the heaven.
The line was crammed with seers and what they glued their eyes on
Was the ranks of the 'REST' as twelve abreast they reached the far
    horizon.

The whistle blew like a saxophone, 'cause Beetham had a cough.
The crowd roared out like thunder. 'Look you beggar, they're off'
Then sinew strove with sinew, like lightning flew the ball,
As Usworth's mighty forwards charged that padded human wall.

MacGregor in the centre had roused his Highland blood,
He put his motor byke flat out and rode them down like mud.
'Scots wha hae wi Watson led.' His weapon cleaved the air.
His exhaust blew off Harold's pants. He played in underwear.

The crowd yelled out 'Hail Usworth. Come let us all rejoice.'
Above the baying of the hounds came Robson's raucous voice,
'Shoot for the goal and take your chance, you'll never get another.
If we get beaten, when I go home I daren't tell my mother.'

Now Harold was their star turn, as lanky as a weed
Legs just like a Skylark's and a damn good turn of speed.
Once he got into his stride t'was hopeless to pursue.
Except of course for Nolan the fastest man we knew.

Tom could turn upon a tanner, and jump ten feet in the air.
He could do a running somersault and never turn a hair.
Harold never saw him come nor saw the ball depart
For Tom could beat the flying Scot and give it two miles start.

The ball shot left and Coulthard rushed ahead like steed into battle,
With push and heave he forged a path like a bus in a herd of cattle.
On, on, went he until he reached the enemy's twenty five,
Then twirled his stick above his head and loosed a sizzling drive.

Straight as an arrow the ball sped on, our Gos took it on the run.
Around the backs it whistled and through the goal it spun.
A mighty cheering rent the air. The crowd all put their bobs on
'We'll break you yet!' said Beetham. Quoth Watson, 'Yes, with knobs on.'

Then off again straight to the right, the oval spheroid flew.
The forwards rushed and slashed and pushed and Elder got it through.
He ran as from a mother-in-law. The crowd stood in a trance.
He tripped and fell upon his face and dirtied all his pants.

Away up to the Usworth goal Beetham on his own.
Then Grimwood flashed into the fray, his stick cut to the bone.
But Harold sprang into the breach, aloft he waved his stick
He seized his chance and underpants and leapt on through the thick
He reached the goal Childe Harold did and found to his dismay
Our smiling back, Miss Walton, she has a taking way.

As for the Rest, they did their best and blew a vulgar razz.

The tumult and the shouting dies, Miss Walton looks the line along
And turning to the Royal Box end she bows unto the splendid throng.
Cool as a tin of Heinz baked beans, she clears the pill. 'Well saved.'
The crowd yelled harder 'Hasn't her hair been beautifully parliament
    waved.'

Alf Coulthard then took up the sphere and forward sped away.
He'd come a bit late and charged the gate, he was driving the B.S.A.
In top he hurtled down the pitch, his bonnet bumped and bored
Like a fireman stood Nan upon the running board.

She smote the rest upon the breast and poked them in the calves
On, on, they drive, past twenty five, the full backs cut in halves.
Upon the circle see them stop and give a sideways glance
Then quick as lightning shoot the ball across to our Nance.

My sister took a mighty swipe, and cut a lot of grass,
The ball sped on to the outside a really top hole pass.
The winger sped and took it well. Bravo for Goodfellow.
Her stick took Beetham in the ear. The crowd's roar drowned his bellow.

Across into the centre the ball came full and hard.
The full back stopped it with his eye, the goal was but a yard.
The goalie got upon his knees as up came Tommy Wood.
He got pneumonia off the breeze and deafness from the thud.

For Tommy was in fighting trim, his drive is something rare.
The ball hit someones stomach with a thud that shook the air.
Out rushed the ambulance brigade, Tom Paul's attaché case.
He plucked the ball from his stomach and said 'Infirmary case.'

'Half time, Half time' old Beetham coughed. The teams turned straight
    around.
The linesmen rushed across, carried the corpses off the ground.
'You'll get it now' said Beetham, 'Don't think my lads are done.'
'On with the ball' quoth Watson. 'My men, the fight is on.'

Then Cooksons seized the flashing pill, the sticks flew in and out.
Miss Elder jumped into the fray and just as slick jumped out.
For mud was flying everywhere, it dirtied her new shorts,
But her yellow jumper shone like gold, she'd come straight from the courts.

Before their glazing eyeballs the bilious garment shone
And 'ere they regained their eyesight she through the goal had gone.
'Three nowt' Young Daisy threw her chest, and all the crowd went mad,
Then threw her English to the winds and yelled 'Noo Howay Lads'

Then raged the battle loud and long, right through the second half.
Old Beetham wouldn't blow off side 'til I kicked his fatted calf.
Ten minutes left he jumped and smote with rage his ponderous paunch
'On Tynemouth, Cookson's Benwell' a human avalanche.

Of flying sticks and flashing studs and dirty coloured socks,
On on they swept, a futile horde, and crashed on Usworth Rocks.
For when they reached the goal line, 'He who dares will die'
Quoth Watson gory stick in hand and murder in his eye.

Then Grimwood hewed that forest of legs till with a mighty crash
His stick head flew and carried away our captain's black moustache.
The Coulthord's struck, the Waltons hacked, The Elder, 'elder own,
The sticks were bent, the air was rent, with sound of wood on bone.

Hail Usworth mightier than the rest, the battle's won at last.
The swooning players fell around, the crowd stood all aghast.
As the whistle blew, the ball rolled from that heaving heap of mince
And Ropper kicked as he can kick. It's not been heard of since.

Toll for the brave that are no more, or words to that effect.
A mighty victory we won, but what did you expect?
'Elementary' my dear Watson cried although we all feel hinny
Admirals all for Usworth Sake, 'The Swingy little thingy.'

Usworth scored three. The Rest nil.

The Three Doddses

This city from most ancient days,
Has been famous for Nottingham Lace.
It's been known for decades,
That Nottingham Maids,
For Beauty must take pride of place.

I have wondered why any one town
Should have won this especial renown,
Why Nottingham girls are the jewels and pearls
That garnish this fair city's crown.

Now to read in the annals and odysseys
Some say they really were goddesses,
But the folks of Bridgend recall a legend
Of a family whom they called the Doddses

From this I've propounded a thesis,
Of Nottinghamshire's female species,
About three of the best, as you might have guessed,
Who happen to be my great nieces.

So let me now tell you the truth
That is stranger than fiction forsooth,
Of the eldest, that's Pam,
And then there's Jo-an,
And the pretty one there who's called Ruth.

Though part of the lore of this town,
They've not spent their lives sitting down,
From the land of their birth they have travelled the earth
And won their fair share of renown.

When Canada's Expo 67,
Was supposed to upstage earth and heaven,
Our answer was 'Pronto! Send Pam to Toronto.'
Of her coming due notice was given.

Warning to Canada

Oh CANADA: Your Rockies, Your lakes and cities fair
That span from far Antarctica to South of God knows where,
Turn over all your Maple leaves, declare a holiday,
You'll have a lot to brag about when OUR PAM gets there.

Oh lucky town TORONTO, the first to know her name,
With shouts of 'Dodd almighty', her coming you'll acclaim.
Your steeples shake with carillon to mark that joyous day,
The sound of acclamation rolls over Hudson Bay.

The trappers in the forests, the miners from the mines,
The fishermen forsake their nets and put away their lines,
The men of far Newfoundland set forth by sled and sail
And twice ten thousand Mounties pour down the Yukon Trail.

The loggers will shout 'TIMBER!' and 'TIMBER!' yet again
At the finest pair of timbers that ever crossed the main.
The Frenchmen shouting 'VIVE LA REINE!' will shake old Quebec's
    walls,
They'll tear the brim off Medicine Hat and stop Niagara Falls.

And as the acclamation dies on that portentous date,
Pam Day becomes a holiday in each Canadian State
To celebrate the coming of Pamela the Great,
You'll make the EXPO 67 seem like a Garden fete.

St. Margarets 1967

The Ballad of St. Cuthbert's Drive

Noo listen aall ye Geordies,
To Caesar lend your lugs,
Pack up your jobs and had your gobs
And I'll brighten aall your mugs.
For here's a modern saga,
'Twill thrill you to the core;
The exile's return to Tyneside
And the jungle of FELLING SHORE.

You've heard of Hilary's Everest,
Columbus discovered the Yanks,
But to Cuthbert's Drive and back alive
Took a fella from Eighton Banks.
Old Gateshead's days were numbered
The Mayor of Gateshead said,
'We'll rub the Felling off the map
And build a town instead'.

'We'll build a new Metropolis
Beside the River Tyne,
'Twill rival Ancient Venice
And cities on the Rhine,
Shanghai upon the Yangtze,
From Khartoum to Irkutsk,
Till Rome upon the Tiber
Looks like Lamesley on the Gut.'

They called up all the architects,
Designers, blokes with plans,
Back room boys and boffins
And all the long haired clans.
They set to work to bring to life
A crazy planner's dream,
The city of St. Cuthbert
New London on the Leam.

And when at last the plans were passed,
Men saw the great design,
A mighty roar rent Felling Shore
And rumbled 'cross the Tyne.
Behold the great Metropolis
Spread-eagled round the school,
The tangled streets ran left and right
Just like a baall of wool.

The Aldermen and Councillors,
The Mayor in splendid state,
Came to the Leam to open the dream
Arriving two days late.
For every bloomin' road they took
To reach that bloomin' school,
Went to the Knowes or Byker Bridge
Or even White Mare Pool.

'I hereby open this City'
His worship said, 'Ahem'
'I offer my chain to the bloke with a brain
Wat knaas of a quick way yem.'
They brought the Town designer
And asked him for a route.
He said 'I only live here
Cos I can't find my way oot'.

'Suppose you take one road apiece
and follow where it goes
Yer bound to come out somewhere,
But where? Law only knows.'
The crowd took up the chorus
'Yes. Follow where it goes
Yer bound to come out somewhere
And the Gud Law only knows.'

The Mayor was hard of hearing
He said 'If CUD LAWS knows
Then fetch old CUD and pronto.
How come LAW only knows?'
Old CUD stepped on the platform,
The Mayor said 'Listen CUD
If you can get me out of here
This chain is yours for good.'

The old man bowed his head in thought
The crowd could hear him think,
The silence fled when someone said,
'Gor Blimey what a stink.'
'A sign! A Sign!' öld Cuthbert yelled

'If to this sign you keep,
Just march along and follow the PONG
We'll come to HEWORTH HEAP'.

All hailed these words of wisdom
Some shouted 'Good old CUD'
And some said other things as well
That people never should.
Then Cuthbert lead the multitude;
Behind him came the band
The Aldermen and Councillors
A hanky in each hand.

The trumpets blew, the banners flew,
The steeples shook with bells.
With grunts and shouts, they blew their snouts
And sorted out the smells.
Then as the smoke got thicker
Some had resort to pegs.
One lot was lost, their trail had crossed
A box of rotten egss.

One contingent came to halt
Beside an old gas main,
Some others walked to PENSHAW
Along an open drain.
Of all the records made that day,
By far the longest trip
Was ten miles in a circle
Around the local tip.

Far in the van, Old Cuthbert ran,
Behind him surged the crowd.
They coughed and choked from dust and smoke
The Lord Mayor wept aloud.
When through the smoke Old Heworth broke
And towered over head,
A mighty mountain belching fire,
Old CUD ran framed in red.

'HAIL FREEDOM' cried the happy Mayor.
The Aldermen all cheered.
'Give thanks to good old CUTHBERT'
But CUD had disappeared.
Intent upon his Mayoral chain
He ran straight for the HEAP
He never saw the gaping maw
Of a stoke hole three miles deep.

And when at last they stood aghast
The smoking crater yawned,
'A Martyr's death' the Lord Mayor said
'Long will old CUD be mourned'
'This day he will be cannonised:
His name we'll keep alive,
The Highway to this city
Shall be St. CUTHBERT'S DRIVE.'

And there it is unto this day
Beneath a purple haze,
THE CITY OF ST. CUTHBERT,
That beats the Hampton Maze.
And for bewildered travellers
When all escape is gone
There's always ELDER'S HOSTEL
At number ONE FIVE ONE.

Golden Wedding Anniversary

May 1943

I remember, I remember, this house where I was born,
When I say 'Home' this picture fills my mind:
Within these walls we laughed and cried, were happy and forlorn,
Then scattered as the chaff before the wind.
And oft returning from the south to see my Mam and Dad,
Like bird of passage on some inborn quest
I came not here, for without them t'was but an empty shell.
The swallow uses not a last year's nest.
But the old birds kept on waiting. As they knew, 'Poor little things
They grow their wings and then they fly away'.
But those little birds are back again with littler ones as well
And Number 5 is home sweet home today.

Yes! Pasture field is home again, each little memory calls,
And we love each little stone from front to back,
But it's not the house that makes this home on this our family day,
But the fact that EVERY little bird's come back.
In this world and in these days that's a Miracle.
The Grace of God; perhaps you call it chance.
We stand here by the Grace of God, and the strength of Tom and Con.
The fortitude of Daisy and of Nance;
To them we stand, to them we owe, all that we have and hold,
Who bravely span the years on bridge of sighs,
And build the fairy fabric of that coming day of days
From the sunshine in young Keith and Barrie's eyes.

For Daisy and my Bonny Nance pull not a Sunday face.
They do not want your sympathy and groans,
The hungry heart has but one food and they would rather fast.
The famished bird blunts not his beak on stones.

They know their task and find their strength
Embodied in the smiling of a son.
This minute is their life complete. In Keith and Barrie's eyes.
Stands smiling Tom and Husky brother Con.
They know for they have bravely watched
The longing years trudge by on leaden feet.
All worldly things are but as mist
And love alone remains concrete.
Learn ye it too and hold it fast,
All other things are loss not gain.
If ye know not, these 50 years,
We celebrate were lived in vain.

These 50 years, these 50 years, these 50 years.
A solemn thought I give it ye again,
Love is concrete if ye know not
These 50 years were lived in vain.
This Elder tree bears yet a smiling blossom
That makes yon corner cot the sunny side
Of streets that oft dishearten care worn neighbours,
We are the seeds. Fall not by the wayside.
We had the joy, inestimable treasure,
To grow beneath its warm and kindly shade.
What did we learn of life and living yonder?
How have we grown? Of what tree are we made?
There is no laurel wreath for steadfast living.
Their well run 50 miles was not for prize
Reward there is, but we must do the giving,
They'll see it in your neighbour's shining eyes.

Had I but served my God with half the zeal,
A Cardinal once voiced his misery,
That I have served my King, would he
Have left me thus in my extremity?
Thus do they wail who lean on princes
To ride them easily up life's steep hill,
So wailed I as a self blind youth
When worldly ambition did outrun my skill.
'Had he but served his family, as his neighbour'
Short sighted insult to his goodness I did groan.
For youth is blind, the blindness of a stone.
Speak not about the heathen in his blindness,
But bear ye yet a while with me in mine.
Their lives proclaimed one song. 'Love ye thy neighbour.'
They cast the pearls. How long was I the swine?
I did but spend one year outside this circle
Finding what a kindly neighbour really is.
And time erased this slur upon his wisdom
By giving me the wisdom to see his.

Nor did he preach to me upon upbringing.
No pious exhortation passed his lips,
He followed closer still a poorer christian
Who bade the twelve disciples leave their ships,
Who never said 'Go ye and tell the people'
Who knew that ears can't hear as well as eyes,
Who scorned the empty windiness of preachers.
'Go ye' He said, not talk, but 'DO Likewise'.
What wisdom lies within that simple statement,
How great the voice that whispers in your ears,
The splendour of that wordless wondrous sermon
We've listened to for these last 50 years.

'Tis strange the things that man will label greatness,
That oft forswear the meaning of the word.
How many seeking self we hear as great men.
How many truly great we've never heard.
How many seeking service to his fellows
In leadership has stepped beyond his plan,
And beckoned by the glitter of position,
Have sought the petty pompousness of man.
That sorry sidetrack never crossed his foot path,
He was too strong to fear to appear weak,
Who might have sat on Aldermanic Benches
Yet shovelled snow. Yea, blessed are the meek.
Nor think ye not t'was but a show of meekness
To prove he never feared his hands to soil,
He never stooped to conquer menial labour,
But raised the dignity of honest toil.

Their time, their health, their lives and goods
Were there, for all who sought them in distress,
They came and went with lighter step
How dear the help had cost they couldn't guess.
Alone of all who knew these kindly christians
We nine could know how great the calls they met,
And this is how their greatest gift was ours
An example that I've not seen equalled yet.
I've heard a preacher talking of God's people
'God's folk are poor' he said to me, and yet,
I knew he didn't know half of the story,
God's folk are not just poor, they are in debt.

These 50 years, these 50 years, these 50 years,
Have plodded down the lane this humble pair.
She wears the splendid emblem of her service
A shining halo wrought in silver hair.
Where'er she walks the smiles of little children
Spring up like daisies shining in the grass.
What honour mine to've been her little laddie,

Oh! sisters mine to've been her little lass.
The nightingale enthralls the stars at even,
His carol from the copse fills night's blue dome,
But the angels stopped to listen to my mother
Singing this little piggie stopped at home.
How lucky I that she has called me hinney
How tenderly she tucked us into bed,
Her goodnight had the richness of a blessing.
Her kiss the hand of God upon my head.

And when we'd grown beyond her ministrations,
And Nance no longer cried for Mammie's care,
She went out to the world still on her mission
And shared her heart with other babies there.
Until one day a laddie called her Nanna,
And others came to greet her now and then.
She took our babies on her knee and hugged them
And started on her mission once again.
And when ye brought your baby to my mother
T'was just like hunger at the sight of food,
No hesitation when those arms were open,
They knew they'd found incarnate Motherhood.
And did ye see them catch my Dad a bending
They know no horse's back is like my Dad's.
I've heard my self when watching Barrie climbing
Say, 'This man was made just right for little lads'.

Mark well this instant child reaction,
These bonny bairns so far from worldly wise.
What have these two that makes the mighty magnet,
That kindles such a light in infant eyes?
Oh! had we but the sight of little children
That sees the spirit through the human form,
He said, 'For they shall be as little children'
They see undimmed these hearts both big and warm.
These two are really yet as little children
To young folk that's the plainest thing to see,
And every bairn that seeks their happy haven
Adds aeons to their immortality.

Mark ye their lustrous eyes, those tears unbidden,
No more of sadness tell than summer rain,
This minute is their joy a taste of heaven,
Man's greatest bliss is garnished oft with pain.
I said 'This day these two do taste of heaven'.
You'll read it somewhere in that ancient tome
'Blessed are they, their reward shall be in heaven'
Their heaven's here and now this very room.
Don't think they're sailing on a sea of Jasper,

They don't hear angels playing harps of gold,
Have I not made it plain they've solved the story
That lies behind that fairy tale of old.

This have I learnt, they've taught me all the scriptures
Unwrapped in parable or prophet's dream,
The Lord won't be annoyed with you for listening
And may he knock me down if I blaspheme.
If Jesus walked, he walked for Nickel Simpson,
His heart was big, He walked for Arnel too.
For Czecks and Poles and Yanks and blokes from Backworth,
For Huns and Hoboes, Saps like me and you,
And when he speaks to me He speaks my language,
How else would He ask that I understand.
His voice sounds not to me like Usworth Rector,
Though I've heard it sometimes in the Colliery band.
When Jesus roamed the earth and told His story
The folks were just like me as dumb as clods
They bumped Him off because He promised Heaven,
What would they've done had he said they were Gods?
He knew they couldn't follow profound wisdom,
Those lads from Gallilee had no fifth form,
He knew the only way to get it over, was,,
To sling the whole thing into story form.

The parable of the sower, the vineyard husband man,
Were tales of men who made those angry mobs.
Just think! he had to hand the keys of heaven
Wrapped up in little tales about their jobs.
But someone must have seen through his devices
To one or two the Master got across.
But many never even took the wrapper off the keys,
Twas, when He died He really got across.
He spoke to those lads in their native language,
If He came here He'd have a Goerdie Twang.
If there's a place in heaven for Hawker Wilson
The Bible should be written out in slang.
'If ye believe' said He. 'All will be added'
That ye cannot believe's the only bar.
You can't because the whole thing is so simple,
You can't believe how fortunate you are.
Those heavens up above with airborne angels
Those parables are sticking in your crop.
You can't get in the door of God's great boundless store,
For the parsons standing there all talking shop.
If you're waiting for a heaven in the boneyard
Your waiting for a train on Bewicke Line,
'The kingdom' (so He said) 'of heaven's within you'
Is that not straight enough for thee and thine?

When I think of how I tried to picture Jesus
I laugh unto myself until it hurts.
I do believe he earned his bread by fishing
How did he manage in those long white shirts?
That is not scorn but just my native language
That I might tell what I do not hold cheap.
If heaven is not paved with human laughter,
Then put me on the road for Heworth Heap.
And our Gregor who has earned her place in heaven
Can you see Ken down at the equipment base
Saying. 'Hev aa got to flee about wi them things?
Wey if aa flap me wings aall rive me claes'
And can you see my Dad when he's in heaven?
Can you all see those flowing robes of white?
'Wey ye taak, me sharts hooked on me feathers.'
A Crown? His bloomin' dut is nivver strite!
Their heaven's here and now this very minute,
If ye would see them live and live again,
Do to your bairns as ye have all been done by
These 50 years will all be lived again.

The Teacher

'I am here as a Member of Parliament because of the influence of one of the finest men it has been my lot to meet in life. He led a class of young fellows and left his mark upon us. Yes, and upon our village. He was well read and able; but it wasn't that which held us, it was the man. "He was a fine man was James Elder."'

I had been listening intently to my fellow M.P. for another County and wondering at the depth of feeling as his words came, but when he mentioned that name I fairly jumped.

'James Elder'

'What like man was he?'

'Short, dark, active, fine head, bushy curly hair'.

I laughed. For James Elder has long been a friend of mine, and every word my Parliamentary colleague uttered was truth itself. The things I could tell about James Elder; born among pits, little education, yet well read, straight as they make them, always a smile and encouragement for you, never seeming to need any himself. Perhaps the greatest gift that can come to any man, is to be able to draw upon the depths of himself, until he runs over with good fellowship for others.

Somehow he makes you forget about your troubles and the things that are going wrong. You meet him and PFFT: things are different. He has taught a few generations of men. Hard work, a family to feed and clothe, a leader among his fellows, deeply concerned in fundamental, social and political matters; wisdom is his possession and a serenity which philosophers seek but do not always find.

Those words of my colleague set me thinking. James Elder and his young men's class. There were once a lot of James Elders and their classes. Some were cultured, some were crude. But it was the men themselves who held us. In towns and villages throughout Britain they held their classes on Sundays, sometimes during the week, asking no pay, gripping their scholars, drawing from deep, deep places the manliness so hidden that none suspected it was there, least of all the possessor.

They left upon their scholars the mark of personality. Now, I wonder if in old Greece there were such men, who worked with their hands, carried upon them the marks of hard labour, and gathered knowledge while they rested, to one end: that they might conduct a class and mould men. Greece had its philosophers we are told, who held their scholars. I know little of these things, but question whether these ones held their scholars more wrapt than the James Elders. But Greece never had such working men as this teacher friend of mine and others like him. They leave their mark upon their community do these men. The community doesn't say aloud, 'Now we mustn't do this or that, because he wouldn't like it'. The fact is, that the personality concerned does not consciously press upon our minds. It is an unconscious quality which pervades us, drawing upwards.

A week or two ago I went to call on my friend. Mrs. Elder was ill, very ill. She was a worthy mother of such a home; they were of the same mould. In fact, for quiet resolute character, covered with laughter and twinkling eyes which made it all seem so easy, commend me to the Elders.

There she lay, pink and white faced, with a veritable cloud of lovely white hair, smiling, joking. You would never dream there was pain. But there was. Pain had left its mark on the shrunken form and thinned face. But the laughter was there still and the twinkling eyes.

A week later she was dead. I went to see my friend. There was no mourning or weeping. Heartaches, of course, we who have lived our years are not to be deceived on that point. But here were no tears.

Mother had asked that a chapter of the Bible should be read. Father said they would do it just as it had been done long ago when the grown sons and daughters were bairns and said their 'pieces' at the Chapel.

So each of the half dozen said two or three verses of the Scriptures they had learned for the anniversary years ago. That made Mother very happy. Then she fell asleep. Tell me, wise one of the world, of any philosophy, reasoning, knowledge, new order anything past or present, that has been known so to sustain the pained one, that she glows with love and happiness while suffering and dying.

'She was a lovely woman', neighbours and friends said. 'He was a fine man', my Parliamentary colleagues said. And her loveliness and his fineness were rooted in the Scriptures. There are people who hardly believe such characters exist. But they do, only we need eyes to see them. Just depends what you are looking for.

One of the marvels of our history, or any other history for that matter was the coming together of this nation in the days of stress. If there is anything more striking, it is the steady insistence on that unity until those who have afflicted the world are utterly blotted out.

It is true we had gone 'dopy' a bit. Let us be frank, we had. But somewhere deep down there was that man and woman whom wrong and injury to others shocked themselves. Peril to the things we unconsciously respect struck home: and the world will remember the result for ever. A great new race was born, or was it reborn? There are exceptions, of course, hardly worth remembering.

The coming age will need the best we have. If we can do on the fields of peace what we have done on the battle fields, we can go gaily to meet the challenges that will surely be thrown down. But it is neither with the economic nor the scientific that the answer lies – it is in the realm of the spirit. Great teachers are needed, even if they are not proclaimed great. Like those who held classes, plumbed the deeps for men and found them. In critical days Greece had her Plato, Rome her Virgil. Men, men, give us men. That was their theme.

We have none such as these. But we have one Jesus, who has shaped men and women for long centuries. He exalts the lonely and works wonders with almost impossible materials. It is to the un-named, the humble that Britain must look as she looked for centuries, to the teachers such as the one of whom I have written.

House of Commons 1945.
by Jack Lawson M.P.

Reverie

The lamp burns dim, the fire's glow,
Sends red and shadows o'er the room,
Outside, the wind blows high
And rain clouds hide the moon.

'Tis chill again, the harvest's in,
And old man Winter totters over yonder hill,
I feel his breath and love that friendly glowing fire,
And shuffle nearer still.

My thoughts fly home to friends I love,
I long to speak and then,
I take a leaf and try to pour my heart out through my pen.

My spirit flies with freedom born of kind regard
And leaves this clay still pen in hand.
Then through the night I flash in thought's brief flight
And walk unseen my own Northland.

The Tees roars 'neath my feet, a stile, a field, a road,
A little bridge, a brook, a cot.
I stand and watch the rosy glowing windows,
I steal to one and see, but am seen not.

A cheery fire leaps the shining bar,
Where Chrissy sits and smooths her silken fur.
A mat frame stretches doorward from the hearth
And that's where I find her.

A grey Madonna, all alone she works and weaves,
Still in her old grey shawl.
Her face a picture of that joy, that springs from
having lived and given all.
And as she weaves her mat a pattern grows before my eyes,
A tale of joy and tears and work and woe and little children's cries.
It is the story of her life, her hopes and fears, her home.
As carefully penned as cloistered monk transcribes some holy tome.

I watch and read the tale as nimble fingers clip and hook and pull.
The happy times are shown in brightest hues,
The sorrows show in shades more dull.
That shining border is the joy of life that's lived as life should be.
Yon sturdy line tells of a task begun and persevered so willingly.

That tree that fills the pattern with her leaves,
Bears fruit she tends with care and love,
The fallen fruit bereaves.
Bright are the blossoms she has woven there,
Each petal fashioned with a mam's own care.
And still she sits and smiles, and loops and pulls.
She turns and stirs the fire and adds some coals.
Then on she goes, the glasses blurr with tears,
A sombre shade weaves in the tale and grows and fades.

She smiles again and takes a brighter patch,
She laughs, I hold my breath and watch.
See! in yon corner near that dark brown place
She's conjured up a funny laughing face.

I laugh myself, we laugh aloud, for see,
I think things at her and she thinks of me.
Unseen I stroll in through the wall and stretch myself upon the butler's bed.
But Chrissy knows, she comes and purrs,
I stroke her head.

And then I cut some clippings from our Jim's old breeks
Or whistle softly to the progger's creeks.
And then I rise and pay some friendly calls
To friends of mine that hang upon the walls.

Straw hat and stick, a massive boulder,
He is as near as though I touched his shoulder.
I pass, and Tucker smiles as though in fun,
And murmurs that his French homework is done.

And Evelyn says 'I've buttoned up my coat'.
And Jim's snore, 'Grunt, plus coo of doves'.
Says, 'Bedclothes fit me like a pair of gloves'.
Downstairs, the fire flicks and dies,
Scarce brighter than old Tibby's glowing eyes.
I pause awhile in dreams and as I stand
A silky muzzle steals into my hand.

I go. The chickens roost, the brook leaps, laughs and tumbles with the
    trout.
The brig, I turn, the upstairs light winks at me and goes out.
And here I am in Herts, it's 12 o'clock,
And I must fly to bed or miss the cock.

Hertfordshire 1935

Wee Magregor – James & Annie Elder with their first three children

The Elder family in 1917
Back Row: Evelyn, Alex, Jenny, Edith, Lily
Front row: James Elder (Father), Daisy, Nancy, Tom, Annie Elder (Mother)

Grandfather & Son John 1909

Grandfather aged 80 1919 (Old Cadknuckles!)

Edith, Mary & Evelyn 1900

Mr & Mrs Elder at their Golden Wedding 1941

The author at work 1960

Self portrait
and wife
Sybil with
grandchildren
sculpted
by author

The author sings with the D.B.C. Orchestra – 1945 in Copenhagen

4th generation Elders

Flowers and Fruits of the Elder Tree

Betula Alba

One Sunday, when all good folk were in Church,
I wandered in a copse and saw a birth,
And this thought came to me:
Oh Birch! How can the beauty be
Expressed, that God expressed in thee?

Is it the artist who with brush and scroll
And one presumptuous stroke proclaims thy bole?
A band of grey? or silver?
'Tis not thy shade.

I see gold and green and red displayed:
Can he, by mixing white and green,
Produce thy glorious leaf and wondrous sheen?
Nay artist, 'tis not thou who canst portray
This Lady Birch's fine array.

In music and the wonderland of sound
For thee my Birch, can fitting notes be found?
Can flute with thin, sweet, trembling trill,
My heart with joy as does your shimmering fill?

Midst symphony and harmony we search,
But sound can not portray the silver birch.
No picture and no sound however fine
Can reproduce the grace that's in thy line.

Thy beauty is unique, to copy it I see.
Ah! Can the poet translate thee
To the base code of A.B.C? Unhappy thought.
No, rhymster, thou canst not. Be off, vain scribbler,
With thy futile rot.

Finchale Woods 1926

69

Cauldron Snout

Up where the Pennine Hills meet with the skies,
Old Mother Nature a recumbent giant lies,
Her brown limbs in a misty blanket rolled,
Her rugged forehead crowned with sunset gold.
From this great Wedlock sky and Mother Earth
With stormcloud labours came a Royal birth.
A 'queen to be' of rivers meant for highest seas.
A moorland princess came, the baby Tees.

Lightly she trips down hill o'er peat
That browns her. Heather makes her sweet,
Where gentians bloom and lambkins leap o'er rugged turves.
Until she stops and peeps o'er Cauldron Snout
And seems to pause like wandering child in doubt,
Then spies the placid dale stretched down below
And fears the leap, yet knows that she must go.

Then Mother Nature from her sleep aroused,
Fearful her child will fall, her misty drowse
Rolls back, and with despairing grip
Seizes the trembling babe from the lip,
Then like the badger sow, when hunter pressed
Devours the squealing offspring at her breast
Hoping to spare it a much harsher fate
Mayhap to be restored some happier date,
This Mother to a raving witch is turned
And in a boiling cauldron Tees is churned.

Beneath the rugged snout that once caressed
The iron jaws bite with a fearful zest,
And as the flood leaps on, mad with despair,
The Snout flings foaming Tees high in the air,
And springing like a deer from prison lair
She crashes headlong down the rocky stair,
The boiling Cauldron's tipped head over heels
And fills the canyon with her thunder peals.

The brown flood drifts along in peace at last,
A foam flecked pebble tells of what is passed.
And as a crowd of children out of school
She chatters home and pauses at a pool.
She thinks and dreams of ships on mighty seas,
And so begins the pleasant Dale of Tees.

Up where the Pennine Hills meet with the skies,
Old Mother Nature a recumbent giant lies,
Her brown limbs in a misty blanket rolled,
Her rugged forehead crowned with sunrise gold.
Turns in her sleep and, as the morning dawns,
Her dewy limbs are wet with tears, she mourns,
Her cry the grouse repeats, it echoes back
As wheeling o'er the Tees he cries, 'Come back. Come back'.

1929

Good God

'Good God' I said,
'A world you made,
Concocted quick from soil and sin
Pure beauty, bestial lust,
Sweet kindliness and cruelty.
Thy tortured image dwells therein.
Bland Patriarch, damned timeless swine.
Not, that you horrors planned
or hatred spawned,
for flies contented dwell
in filth and maggots death,
seeing no further than
the life's brief span,
but MAN thine image
Oh hast thou no heart?
Crawls in his murky minute,
whilst, he has the sight
of aeons hence.
Milleniums mock his agony,
Utopia gleams beyond his topmost rung.
What cruel cynic torturer refined
to grant the vision
and withhold the time?'

'Shortsighted fool' God did reply.
''Tis the whole plan
that he should live
his fleeting minute
as a futile man,
with yet that picture
in his eye
that will be human
in the bye and bye.

'Tis his to see
for generations not yet known.
His is to strive,
for what can't be his own.
Did he but this
strive selfless for a year,
his soul would live
beyond his utmost fear
of his
mortality.'

Teesdale 1930

Song of the Morning

Blessed am I of all mankind
Though not for goods or gold,
For all I have is freely given,
For all mankind to hold.
For glorious life and burgeoning earth
Sun warmed from east to west
Is mine, because I know who gives
And know that I am blest.

Great sun that sheds His grateful smile
In pageantry at dawn,
Majestic Herald of the day,
A brand new morn
Sweeps o'er the wooded countryside
Trailing a fringe of song,
Spun by a galaxy of larks
The pasture land along.

White pigeons wheeling in the sun
That clap their wings for joy,
A dog's gay challenge up the lane
The whistle of a boy,
Cheerfully bound for his first job,
Has lost his school bound lurk.
High stepping heels adorn the path
Young ladies off to work.

These are the country sights and sounds
That magnify the morn,
And set a man about his task with heart and mind new born.
Yet ere I pass the garden gate and start upon my way,
There comes the most important thing that really starts the day.
I stop and look back up the hedge to where the lattice swings
My lady love has come to wave, that's when my day begins.
Then is my heart with courage filled, thrice blessed am I
I know.
Her love goes with me all the day
Wherever I may go.

Gt. Gaddesden 1960

The Great Gaddesden

Full many English cities proud do boast that where they stand
They stood in William's day 1066.
What paltry lineage! Roman soldiers paddled in the Gade,
And stands our village Church on Roman bricks.

Stand ye at Gaddesden Cross and view this valley of the Gade,
A pastel pastoral where ere ye look.
And every winding country lane that leads to Gaddesden Row,
Was once a boundary line in Domesday Book.

Stand with me yonder in the dusk and watch the Chiltern Hills,
Their bosky brows merge with the evening sky.
Our ancient village is unique, a brand of rustic charm
That even history could not pass by.

The blue smoke from the hamlet ascends the wooded hill,
The Church bell bids the lonely owl to roam,
The Broad Waters couch the moon and still the little Gade
To give the stately swan his island home.

And where we stand the Romans stood, a mailed Centurion,
Would scan the view and halt his weary band,
Retrace his mighty pilgrimage back to his native Rome
Without recalling once a fairer land.

The Ancient Briton crouched beneath the father of Hill Wood
And watched the mighty cohorts marching north,
As would his children's children and many yet unborn,
Take refuge there when Cromwell's men rode forth.

His Lordship from the Manor has cantered down the park
And reined in here his acres to admire.
He saw the rolling cornlands; he watched the grazing kine
And knew he had a gem of Hertfordshire.

He fostered all our Rural Crafts, our fruitful fields and farms
And when Crusading, left it to his sons.
They planted Beech and English Oak. Their earnest husbandry
Foretold the honest labours of the 'Bunns'.

A Hambley Parker once came here, four thousand miles from home.
By happy chance of hers and our fate,
She stood and viewed in detail with a practised artist's eye,
Great Gaddesden, and she knew why it was Great.

Tempted by the river, she was welcomed by the Swans,
Thatched barn, old school, flint church so it appears,
By inn and farm and sunken lane, was beckoned up the hill.
She looked, and loved, and lived there, thirty years.

Bill Mortimer's as fine a son as Gaddesden ever knew,
His signs of office were his fingers green,
If it could grow Bill grew it, his spirit lives here still,
His monument, the beauty you have seen.

The Hambley Parker garden smiled and blessed the passer by,
The almond trees in bloom caressed the lane,
And every flower that ever grew has grown upon Top Hill,
Her coming brought our little village fame.

Don't go to Kew in Lilac Time, Just climb up to Top Hill
In springtime just as April marries May,
The tulips stand like bridesmaids in deep Forget-me-not
And the almonds throw confetti on the way.

So here's to 'Gaddesden's Flower Girl,' We wish her Bon Voyage.
As long as Almond Blossom decks Top Hill,
As long as there's a garden in an English country lane
There'll be a Hambley Parker with us still.

September

We stand on a hill
In Hertfordshire
My love and I,
And watch
September
Steal into
Our Chiltern woods,
And know
That we must go
Where
The untiring sea
Her silver lace
Doth endlessly unfold
Upon
The golden shore,
And the yellow dunes
Reach up
To embrace
The great
Brown green
Hills of Devon.

After Woolacombe 1966

April Showers

Oh! to be in England
Now that April's there,
And whoever walks in England
Finds some morning un-aware,
That the lowest boughs on the brushwood sheaf
Have a bucket of water in every leaf
For the nut who swings on the orchard bough
In England now.
And after the rain the snow follows,
The drifts build up and hide the hollows.
Beware, my blessed pear tree in the hedge,
Leans to the road and splatters you all over.
Icicle dew drops like a razor's edge,
That's a wise bush, he splatters you twice over
Lest you should think that he was only joking
With that first freezing soaking.
And though you're nipped by bitter winter's claws,
You'll be a damned sight colder when it thaws.
You know what you can do with your May flowers
If you'll just spare me all these April Showers.

The Dear Old Soul

When summer brings the townfolk to the country,
I sometimes find among those pleasure bent,
Some dear old soul who'd like to see the poultry
A half hour showing around is time well spent.

'I've seen those other farms you know,
That've just got cows and things,
But never seen a farm that just kept hens.
So just as I was passing, I saw your notice board
And thought I'd come and see them in their pens.'

'What? Don't you keep your hens in pens?
You keep them in a house?
In here, you say? Well, bless me, Sir, you're right.
In cages like canaries! Whoever would have thought?
But where do they all go to sleep at night?'

'Oh yes, I see. They lay an egg, and then it rolls down here,
And if that wasn't there the eggs would fall.
GOOD GRACIOUS! Look at all these here!
You say you have some more?
It beats me how on earth you sell them all.'

'And this is where the chickens live?
Now aren't they simply sweet!
I think they're lovely when they're small like that.
What's that? They've got a lamp in there?
Well now, that's something new,
I thought that's where the chickens' mother sat.'

'And this is where you hatch them. But
What's this cupboard for?
They hatch in there? I can't believe it's true.
They have no mother hen at all, you say?
Poor little dears
It shows you what 'lectricity can do.'

'So what's an incubator? Well!
Whoever thought of that?
I 'spose they hatch out in a day or two?
They don't? They take the same time as a hen?
Well what's the good of that?
You might as well have hens then. MIGHTN'T YOU?'

Reluctantly she leaves at last.
'And thank you for the eggs.
They're different from the sort of eggs you buy,
Goo'day, sir. I've enjoyed my visit very very much.'
'Goo'day', I say.
'You're welcome, so have I'.

St. Margaret's 1938

The Bull Ring

My life has been spent on farms and gardens. Some years ago I went to seek a job as gardener at a dairy farm near Berkhamstead. I was held up in the narrow Fields End Lane by an enormous herd of Ayrshire cows, being driven home to milking by an irascible little man with a big stick and an even bigger vocabulary.

After the successful conclusion of my interview the manager John Webb showed me round the farm. The milking parlour was a clinical eye opener. The cowman I'd met in the road (answering to the name of Bob) was bossing and swearing at his assistants and the Ayrshires were streaming out to the lane back to pasture.

Eventually we came to a large yard with a massive 4ft. brick wall topped by a double rail of 2½ inch steel bars.

'What do you think of him?' said John proudly as my eyes came to rest on the stupendous and majestic bull. 'LESSNESSOCK CREAM MARK' the head of the famous Fields End herd stood like a statue, his nose pointed in the direction of the departing herd.

Three quarters of a ton of Scottish beef. His head was as big as a wheel barrow and his eye had a depth that spoke of patient dignity, despite the ring of servility that hung from his nostrils.

Mark totally ignored our presence and as the lowing of the departing herd faded, he took a deep breath and let loose a roar that echoed right across the Bourne Valley. 'He's magnificent! Absolutely stupendous!' I enthused. 'And we never take liberties with him,' said John solemnly.

A month or two later in search of some well rotted manure for the roses I drove my old utility and trailer into Lower Meadow where there was a three year old clamp. A beautiful day, the steep meadow falling away into the Bourne Valley, I worked in full sun and by the time I was half loaded I was stripped to the waist. It was soon after this I realised I

81

had company. Cows are full of curiosity and they ambled up the slope in twos and threes to inspect this unusual vehicle. There is something beautiful and wholesome about Dairy Cows. The soft eyes, the gorgeous eyelashes, the sweet chlorophyll laden breath. Was not their grandmother called Clover Mist?

Soon I was shoulder high in cows and the late comers pressed forward until I could no longer wield a fork. One Lady, scenting the salt of perspiration, licked my back with a tongue like a door mat. When one of my guests started rubbing on the Utility, the creaking body work told me enough was enough.

'Come on girls!' I shouted, slapping rumps with a shovel, 'Get going!' I moved one, another took its place and in desperation I whacked the back of the car breaker. I was totally ignored. I whacked harder till the head turned slowly revealing a large ring in the nostrils. What passed between Mark and I, I don't remember for in the time it takes to read this sentence I fought my way out of the herd, ran fifty yards and dived under the barbed wire.

After half an hour the herd lost interest and wandered back down the meadow. Mark studiously ignored me to my utter chagrin but I did fancy his departing backside gave me a waggish wave.

My story was a big laugh on the farm. 'Never take liberties with Mark,' said John seriously.

'I only speak to Mark from a Tractor Cab,' said old Ned. 'You're not afraid of this great softie,' sneered Bob the cowman when we met in the yard. Bob held a four foot pole firmly in both hands. At the end of the pole was a ring and firmly attached to the ring was the Mighty Mark. Built on the same lines as an Oxo Cube he looked enormous against the preposterously little man.

'You got to hold his head high,' said Bob. 'He can't charge you without lowering his head.' He jerked the pole upwards and Mark tip toed to ease his tender nostrils.

'You got to show him who's boss.' Mark looked down at me as they ambled off. It seemed the Royal Patience was wearing thin.

It seemed Mark was best controlled when with the herd. He could be driven anywhere. Penned in his yard he got bored and his great bellow rolling out across the farm was a feature of Fields End that everyone got used to.

I was cutting a hedge in the garden one day when the note of the bellow changed subtly and suddenly became a terrible roar. It was an ominous sound and it seemed logical that when it stopped a fearful scream for help followed. Somehow this had all been expected. As I climbed the fence and ran I asked God to show me what to do. The roar and screams beckoned me as I ran. A glance showed Bob, head bloodied, crouching in a corner beneath the wall and Mark's great head crashing against the bricks above him. As Mark backed off for another charge I climbed on the wall shouting and waving my arms to distract him. At my shout he flung up his head towards me and the pole shot into the air to descend into my stretched hands. I jumped back off the wall, knelt and levered his nose down to the top bar. He was my prisoner.

By a fluke he had surrendered himself bound to the enemy. We faced each other eyeball to eyeball through the stout rails as my yells brought the men who carried Bob out. He was not seriously hurt. I thanked God for my instructions. They were just as clear as Mark's. On the following day Mark was to be photographed with an elderly couple, the farm owner and his wife. This was cancelled.

Independence Day

'Hello stranger.'

'Who is it?'

'We've got a visitor.'

'Well bring them in, dear!'

'It's not a them, it's an it.'

The kitten paused on the step, examined us thoroughly, walked through the kitchen, around the lounge, sniffed my slippers, rubbed at my wife's legs, sprang onto a chair, gave a minute nasal inspection to my work pullover, sat down on its haunches and gazed from one to another, with what could have been nothing but approval.

Ever the hostess, my wife poured a saucer of milk.

'Is that wise dear?'

'At the rate it's disappearing it was a crying necessity!!'

Without as much as a thank miaouw, our visitor hopped on the door step and stalked away up the garden path, but I did somehow feel that the tip of the tail waved a little as it passed through the gate.

Our visitor called at very spasmodic intervals, a week, two months perhaps, accepting food, a lap and departed as before.

'Nina says that cat belongs to No. 3. She's called Mary.'

'Yes, Nina says it feeds at every house in the village.'

Our visitor was about half grown the following summer when, after we had almost forgotten her, she walked in looking decidedly the worse for wear. She drank thirstily, ate everything we put down but refused utterly to be picked up or even touched. Licking her whiskers she walked out, looked up and down, paused and came back in, straight through to the lounge which she inspected, article by article until her nose reached positively to my old woollen sweater on a chair. Describing three perfect circles she fitted her tail carefully into its groove and slept all day. My wife renamed her Ginny, and Ginny was with us for a whole week by which time she had her own dishes in the kitchen and I had lost my old pullover.

One Saturday afternoon we were having a cup of tea and Ginny, having finished her saucer, climbed back on the settee for a wash and brush up, when a knock came at the door.

'Have you got our cat? We've been away on holiday three weeks and just got back. Nina says our Mary's been staying with you.'

An eight year old girl followed my wife into the room.

'Yes, that's our Mary!'

But Mary was unrecognisable, her back was arched, her hair on end and as the girl reached, she spat and swore like a bargee.

'OOH!' she said, 'Come on Mary.' But a flashing claw made her draw back hastily.

'I'll go and fetch Daddy.' She trotted off.

'She must have had a dog's life up there, Tom.'

'A dog's life and a three kids' life, I reckon. Then they throw her out while they go on their blinkin' holidays!!'

'Do you want to bet on it?'

'Shut up, here he comes!'

Ginny was standing up on my old pullover when Daddy arrived and she was still standing there when he left with a badly lacerated hand.

As the door closed behind him our eyes met with a decidedly triumphal glint as we went back to the lounge. Ginny was washing herself.

'Well done, Ginny,' I said patting her. 'OW!!'

Next day my wife reported that two boys came with a cat basked for Ginny, saying, 'Our Dad says Mary has got to be put to sleep.'

'And what did you say, dear?'

'I told them to send their Dad for her.'

'She's too wild *for little boys.*'

Ginny has been with us four years. Now and again she climbs into my lap and snuggles into my armpit. Sometimes she gives me a vote of confidence by sinking her teeth into my hand without piercing the skin and looking me straight in the eyes. I think this means 'WATCH IT!'

My grandchildren all have pet cats they treat like dolls at home. One of them has been known to sit still for an hour and a half when Ginny honoured her by sleeping on her lap.

'When is Ginny's birthday, Nana?'

'I think it must be the 4th of July.'

We Plough the Fields and Scatter

Having worked on the land all my life, I am a peaceable man and the machines of war have never held a high place in my affections, except one. Having crept slowly behind the English sappers with their Hoover-like metal detectors as they searched for enemy mines, it was with great joy we beheld the first American Flail Tank bowling across the minefields, like a mighty mechanical octopus lashing the ground into thunderous submission.

After the war, back on the farm, the laborious daily chore of shovelling away four tons of poultry manure was suddenly cancelled by the arrival of none other than the direct descendant of the Flail: the mechanical muck spreader whose lashing chains could spread two tons of muck over half an acre in five minutes.

How dependent a farm is on its tractor can only be realised by trying to think of a method of persuading 36,000 chickens to postpone their daily deposits.

How then would you feel at 7 am on a cold, wet Sunday morning, preparing to spread, when your tractor refused to move? Main bearing gone!!

The cleaners calling for an empty spreader, the muck piling up, feeding and egg picking obstructed. Dead stop on a Sunday morning is a fate worse than death.

I grabbed a car and roared off to borrow a neighbour's tractor while the phones behind me rang for help.

It was raining hard and cleaning was at a standstill when I crept back up the farmyard with Dave Simmonds' old Massey Ferguson. Backing up for a hitch I shouted to Andy to chalk up the new road number of the back plate.

The take off brought loud cheers from the cleaners for nothing seemed to work properly. The power take off was decidedly shaky.

I put the tractor into second and turned up the wick as I climbed the hill through the sleeping village, past the row of parked cars. The noise was such that I anticipated some rude remarks from my sleeping neighbours later. In fact, the noise of the old tractor was so great that it almost drowned out the sound of the pelting rain! OR DID IT?!! OR WAS IT?!!

I looked over my shoulder and saw to my horror a great shower of chicken muck spraying over the hedge. STOP!! STOP!! The damned power take off had slipped into gear. I jumped out and ran back.

The cars were all the same colour!! A rather dun shade to coin a phrase. Running back to the spreader its newly chalked index number seemed cruelly apt – PONG 100.

It was no good standing there. My instant reaction to disaster is to PRAY. I prayed and God turned up the rain to fall cats and dogs.

I jumped into the old Massey and with one foot jammed on the power take off I belted off into the field and spread so fast the muck crept over the meadow like a grey mist.

Still praying I drove back down through the village. God was still washing the cars but the road was a sea of brown mud.

With two boys and a broom each we ran back up the street. The downpour was easing but a torrent of water roared down the verge and carried away the slime as we brushed it in. No-one every knew how the street had been fertilised except one neighbour, Roy Morgan, who had an open sports car. I paled as he approached. 'Good job I put the car in the garage last night, Tom. It didn't half come down.' I just had to tell him how right he was!

My Wife's Pans

Thus spoke the good *St. Pancreas*, a sage who knew his book,
'Man doth not live by bread alone be it his wife can cook.'
Read, mark and inwardly digest that girlish ways and wiles
On hungry man fall without heed, whilst *Pies* engender smiles.

When summer suns their langour spread, no kiss comes up to *Jelly*,
'Tis truly said a husband's heart is right inside his belly
And, would ye keep your husband's love and care and every look,
Full many things there are to do, the first of these is *Cook*.

'Variety', it has been said, 'is the great spice of life'.
That's why old HEINZ'S 57 appeals so to a wife.
Be not this common error yours, of all the deadly sins,
How many girls have loved and lost because they opened tins?

This silly rhyme is not for you, My Fair, in person meant.
To women folk in general 'tis, and their enlightenment.
Did I not love you for yourself, your tender way of looking,
At all times lovely in my eyes, I'd *LOVE YOU FOR YOUR COOKING*.

To the best cook in Hertfordshire
Great Gaddesden 1935

The Marlin Saga

All ye aspiring scribes give heed,
Whilst I hold forth on what you need,
And that, my dears, without a doubt,
Is that you should at once find out
How fortunate you all must be
To join this select company.
For doubt it not, in years to come
Your conversationary plum
Will be relating how of yore,
(Note how your listeners all say 'CAW')
You came with eager glance and treat
To Castle Hill in Berkhamsted.
To partake of, as you may see,
The finest hospitality.
For, scour the earth, there is no like
Of gracious Hilda and her Spike.

How this great pair should chance to meet
Coincidence so hard to beat,
The gist of which I now will break
If you will kindly stay awake.
The venerable Spike you know today
A noble son of U.S.A.
A robust Yank to England came
In his own words, 'To pull a dame'.
'I'm looking for a pedigree
Long founded in the old countree'
The beauteous Hilda soon he spied
And in a flash was by her side.
'My dear,' he said, 'In fact, my Darlin',
My nickname's Spike, my surname's Marlin.
You are a lady fair to see –
the Bulldog Breed – Old Family.
Your name goes back for mile on mile.'

Quoth Hilda, 'Been here quite a while.'
Said Spike on bended knee, 'Here goes –
Accept my hand, my English Rose.'
Quoth Hilda, 'English Rose – I'll shock 'im –
I'll have you know my name's Van Stockum,
And I will thank you very much,
To know that I am very DUTCH
And let me say it very loud,
Of which I am immensely proud.'
Then Spike in haste to make amends,
Cried 'Madame, pray let us be friends.
Your golden hair, your Oo La La,
I should have known were from Pays Bas.
What brings you here I'd like to know?'
Said Hilda, 'Aren't the English slow!
The average British man and wife
I often paint and call "Still Life" '.
'You paint?' said Spike 'An artist, you!!'
'I do some landscapes, portraits too?'
'Gee whiz,' said Spike, 'and such good looks.'
Quoth Hilda, 'Have you read my books?'
'Say Ma'am,' cried Spike, 'Can this be true?
A pin up blonde and genius too.
I'm telling you I am bewitched.
What say tomorrow we get hitched?'
'Well now,' said Hilda, 'that takes two.
What say I get the news on you.'
'Say kid,' said Spike with beaming smile,
'I've gotta say I've made my pile,
I've humped that bale in New York docks.
I like to mend Grandfather clocks.'
Said Hilda, 'Tell me what's your views
On five card Bragg and bootleg booze?'
'Say Babe, I'm not that kinda guy.
Shuv Ha'penny is for me too high.
Just look at me. I like to think it,
Wine connoisseur – but never drink it.'
They pledged their troth in dilute lager,
And so began the Marlin Saga.
The exact date I do not know,
It must be ninety years ago.
And in that time they've crossed the Main,
The States, Toronto, back again.
They even say they've dwelt awhile
As natives of the Emerald Isle.
And what a family they have raised,
Still spread world wide – you'd be amazed.
Olga a mission in Africa runs,

Bridget's renaissance is going great guns,
In Canada Randall has climbed to the Peak,
The school of young Sheila expands week by week,
John in New York is a business head,
And Liz is a doctor here in Berkhamsted.

Now that's an achievement in anyone's tongue.
May God bless these Marlins and keep them both young.
We share in their circle, partake of their zest.
I deem it an honour to come as a guest.
So be ye upstanding – the toast if you like
You cannot say better – To Hilda and Spike!

Christmas 1985

Whirlwind Romance

I'm only a simple old Geordie man
As anyone here will observe.
I know I'm not anything special
And that most folks get what they deserve.
So that's why it strikes me as funny,
That angels had me down as worth,
When they opened the windows of heaven
And tipped all their presents on earth.

I only know I was so lonely
Because I'd not lived on my own.
I asked the good Lord for his favour,
And he didn't just get on the phone,
But out in the box with my letters
Was a note that positively shone,
With Love from a Lady at Bromyard
And I heard myself say, 'That's the one!'

I looked up in the sky and said 'Thank You.
I'll go up there now if you like.'
And a voice from on high said 'Elder!
Off your bum, lad, and get on your bike.'
I pointed the Honda at Worcester
And shoved my foot down on the floor,
I just passed a couple of Squad Cars
But the Sergeant swore blind it was four.

'Twas a quarter to nine in Old Bromyard,
Of citizens there weren't too many,
But they all did a bunk down the High Street
As I screamed to a halt at the 'PENNY'.
A note on the door read 'OPPIT,
Can't you see that the whole place is shut!!'
So I gave it a punch with my elbow
And then I let fly with my foot.

The whole place was dark as a chimney,
I tripped and fell over the mat.
There stood two ladies a looking
As if I was something brought in by the cat.
I asked 'Is either of you Mrs Young?'
They only answered with stares,
Till the young one said, 'Mummy, say *something*'
And the other said, 'Get up them stairs!'

The stairs were so dark and so narrow
I said 'Why did they make them so steep?'
And Jessie said 'Keep your hair on,
The next flight's so bad we must creep.'
At last we came to her apartment,
'Is there anyone higher?' I asked.
'There is one more flight,' Jessie answered,
'But you'll require an oxygen mask.'

Don't tell me they live in the attic
I reckon they all must be mad,
'The one up above is Almighty,' she said,
'And don't you forget it my lad.'
I forget how we passed that first morning
But I know we were getting on well,
When a voice from the kitchen yelled 'STARTERS!'
And your mother exclaimed, 'Oh B.L.'

In surprise I said, 'I beg your pardon'
And stood up and reached for my hat,
But the Lady just laughed as she made for the stairs,
Saying 'Oor Albert that taught me all that.'
All hell was let loose in the kitchen,
As I left Jane was too pushed to look,
But yelled, 'My love and prayers will go with you
So you might as well just take your hook.'

I asked what she meant, what's the angle.
I can't make head or tail out of that.
Jess said 'Jane thinks that you are an angel
So just keep it under your hat.'
And so ended our first encounter
As I drove back to Old London Town,
As I opened the door the phone started to ring
And I heard as I lifted it down.

'Is that you at home now, my darling?
What a pity it started to rain.
I hope that you had a nice journey
And when are you coming again?'
'Yes it's me dear,' I managed to answer

As I summoned a very wan smile,
'I don't think I'm coming tomorrow
It's bloody near 400 mile.'

'There was no need for that,' she said shortly,
'I can't think why you make such a fuss,
If you think it's too far to come in the car,
Catch a train or come up in the bus.'
As I stopped at the Penny next morning
Jessie shouted, 'You're out of your head.'
I said, 'You had better get cracking,
Tomorrow we're going to get wed.'

'Don't be so absurd – it's impossible
And I've nothing to wear,' she replied.
'That's going to be tough, Mrs Young,' I called out
'It's 40 below here outside'
The world is made up of tomorrows.
Raise your glasses, your hands, let's say 'Cheers'.
I will always take care of your mother,
You will always be welcome here.

We've just lived a few days in this palace
The workmen just gone down the road,
We looked at each other, 'We've done it!!'
And laid down a mighty big load.
And this is our first real reception,
A reunion that won't be the last,
My wife's playing host to her family,
This is more than just a REPAST.

The Ballad of St. Margaret's Camp

This school was built back in the Thirties,
They called it a camp if you please,
T'was built 'neath the Battle of Britain
For London town's evacuees.

It was built by the fellows from Gaddesden,
From Hemel, The Row, and Berkhamsted,
From Luton and Dagnall and Boxmoor
And a Foreman from London called Fred.

He was big, fat and florid and forthright,
A man not afraid to meet trouble,
The pundits have said that a spade is a spade,
Well to Fred it was 'a bloody great shovel!'

Some called him Steb and some Stebbo,
And some called him names best unsaid,
We were not at a loss to know who was boss
So we called him the Guvner instead.

He pinned up his plans in an office
With windows north, east, south, and west.
'Wherever you are I can see you,
You haven't come here for a rest!!'

There were vapour trails in the Hertfordshire sky
And he gave them a glance as he spoke,
'We're not here to knock up a holiday camp,
It's to get those kids out of the smoke.'

I remember he showed us the ballast,
And a ruddy great mountain of sand –
'The machines are all building walls on the coast
So you're mixing all this lot by hand!!

'And if you're all wondering what tools are to hand
Don't come to the office of works,
'Cos there isn't as much as a trowel to be had
So bring your own shovels and forks.'

His ganger was Johnny from Dublin,
He'd eyes in the back of his head,
If you bent in your trench for a minute
He yelled, 'Fill it in – that one's dead.'

It was forty below when we got the word go
And I went out to cut the first sod,
And Paddy said 'Tom, it'll take a big bomb
To dent that old turf there, be God.'

I said 'Listen, Mick, yer making me sick
Yer a shame to the land ye were born.
Just give me a shovel and without any trouble
I'd shift all the mountains of Mourne.'

Once the job was begun, workers came on the run
No shortage here of man power.
They came for the pay and they came here to stay,
It was now fourteen pence to the hour.

Trenches were dug, foundations were laid
And buildings shot up at the double.
Your feet didn't drag when you ran into snags
The Guvner was there to shoot trouble.

He had a great knack of patting your back
Then kicking your feet out from under.
I've seen a bloke's eyes light up with surprise
Then turn round and work just like thunder.

The navvies on drains weren't helped by the rains,
'Is it over your shoes?' Stebbo said,
'You've seen nothing yet. Tomorrow I'll bet,
Those toilets will come into use.'

There were brickies in tears who couldn't build piers
The Guvner soon sorted their trouble.
He said 'Wot the devil! Is't you or your level?
Don't say there's a kink in the bubble?'

He craftily fostered a feeling of pride,
And rivalry knowing it feels
A carpenter's itching to finish a job
If a painter comes fast on his heels.

He'd say to a chipp 'Now that's looking good
You'll be finished tonight it would seem.

Why not? Listen mate. I would if 'twas me
Or tomorrow they'll paint you all green.'

And down at the Pub on a Saturday night,
The back chat and beer flowing free,
The points on the darts were not half as sharp
As the sting in the old reparteee.

The painters were driven at terrible speed
By a fella they knew as their 'coddy',
One chap a bit old dropped dead of a cold,
His mate just wiped his brush on the body.

No lower form of life exists
Than a plumber – unless it be laggers,
And nothing smells worse than a painter, of course,
Unless it be two of the beggars.

As I walked by a trench came a shower of 'FRENCH'
The air turned as blue as the sea,
'Twas a ruddy great Mick who had just bounced his pick
Off a pudding stone six foot by three.

He said 'You can talk of your soft Chiltern Chalk,
Sure it's flints that would make your heart break.
I came here to work with a new Irish fork,
Look, begorra, it's down to a rake.'

St. Margaret's camp was build on time
But how we know not still,
Unless it was just the high morale
And Stebbo's iron will.

As soon as there was bed and board
Amidst great jubilation.
Two hundred and forty Cockney kids.
To our consternation,

Were swarming over all the site
And belting through the woods,
Said Stebbo with a misty eye,
'It does you bloody good.

'And when they all get settled in
And all is done and said,
We'll hand the whole thing over
And paint St. Margaret's red.'

And of that great and final binge,
Fate surely had last laugh,
For I was many miles away
Square bashing in the R.A.F.

Leave without Absence

Should you at any time in your career have been a member of that august body known as his Majesty's Royal Air Force there is little doubt that you have experienced that unpleasant feeling known to the vulgar as 'Being Cheesed'. The state of cheesdom is one result of having time on one's hands and nothing on one's mind, and the highest degrees of cheesdom have been attained while stationed in Blighty, particularly at one of these outlandish, god-forsaken dromes based on a one pub Metropolis such as Grating on the Wick, Littledoing.

The thing is to have a hobby. There's darts, Waafs, Wallop, Educational Classes and lots of others but for a really interesting hobby give me 'Leave Without Absence.' I don't mean just succumbing to the urge for home and taking off for the station; you may strike lucky but it's a pound to a pinch, that Corporal S.P. at Victoria will ask you for your pass and it's seven days jankers without the option.

Any mug can get jankers and if there's one type who binds me rigid, it's the twerp who brags about how many days he has done.

No, if you are going to tussle with the Police then use your loaf and never, repeat never, travel without a pass. There are several different ways of obtaining leave passes.

1. You can ask the Sarge for a day off. This method is absolutely fool proof but not often successful.

2. You can use an old pass.

Some enthusiasts work on old passes altering dates and I have seen some threadbare old 295's that have got their owners through Victoria across London and all the way back. The risks are high because the S.P's themselves are using similar amateurish methods for the weekend, besides if you have to wait ten days to make the Ist. into the IIth., it's a dead loss because it may be raining.

3. The best method is to make your own complete brand new pass for each excursion. The snag is the orderly room date stamp. If you happen to be an orderly room type, this is a piece of duff. I knew one chap who used to incur jankers regularly in the hope they'd leave him to sweep out the orderly room on his tod. When it paid off he stamped up a selection of dates for the coming season. Nice work! The snag of course was the jankers, which was a two fold disadvantage for they always watch a jankers bird. It's only your pure souled high minded youth who can go missing for a few days without being missed.

Of course the real enthusiast makes his own orderly room date stamp. One needs to be reasonably efficient at lino cuttings. (I was taught it by our handicraft instructor.) A variable date stamp cost 5/6 at any Smiths and when fitted into your lino cut, Bob is your uncle.

Now all passes must be signed by an officer. The overcoming of this snag has been too much for many of my otherwise bold companions, but as I have said, 'Only a chump would forge an officer's signature.' It's best to do an indecipherable squiggle, for it is no secret, the calligraphy of many officers is on a par with their other attainments (if they can write).

To make a really good job of a pass, buy yourself a few bottles of coloured ink and use different pens for the various characters who contribute to your efforts. Flt. Lt. Dead Loss has been a great friend to me in many delightful 'Leave Without Absence,' along with Squadron Leader Michael Mouse D.F.C. and countless other celebrities. The most interesting times for travel are naturally during travel bans such as the authorities love to impose during public holidays.

Full instructions for circumventing these bans are usually published in D.R.O's such as 'All passes must be endorsed in red ink with permission to travel by rail.' A good quality red ink costs 7½d, sufficient for about 15 years. Working on these lines you are bound to have months of trouble free travel. With a really well got up effort in your pocket you can stare out even the most hardened S.P.'s on railway barriers for they cannot face a smart looking type without that 'Stop me and buy one' look.

I remember once skipping off on a crafty forty eight and, doing my customary invisible slink from the gents toilet to a moving third class compartment, I slumped down in a corner seat opposite a passenger engrossed in a newspaper. To my horror I realised he was wearing R.A.F. officer's uniform.

After what seemed four years at least he lowered the newspaper and I looked into the bright blue eyes of our station Warrant officer.

I am sure we both did a double take, only his didn't show too much. With a blinding flash of intuition I guessed he had been doing the 'invisible man' trick behind the newspaper. I decided to go in and bat. Before he could speak I handed him my precious copy of Reader's Digest with a casual 'Care to borrow that Sir? I've read it.'

'Why thank you, Sergeant,' he blurted out, rising to the bait of the highly coloured cover, 'be sure you get it back.' This left me with nothing to read but my iron rations. I pulled from my tunic pocket the tiny New Testament sent me by the Women's Institute of our village. An influx of passengers at the first stop mercifully filled the aching void between us and we lapsed into that abysmal silence that passes for conversation in an English train. On the run to Victoria I was conscious of being put through the toughest inspection I have ever endured, but as St. John aptly stated 'Ye shall pass through the fire and it shall not kindle upon you.'

Had I not upon me the armour of the righteous? Was not my uniform pressed to perfection? Were not my back and sides trimmed to a sparsity that would make Yul Brynner look like an old English Sheep Dog? Was not I wearing an issue soft collar instead of the semi-stiff Van Heusen affected by Smart Alecs?

Did not the albratross on every button stare back at him with brazen brilliance? I had even foregone the flippant Fighter Command one-upmanship of the undone tunic button. The only thing he could have faulted me on was my forage cap set at thirty degrees to starboard compared with his regulation dead centre.

He was down to the last page of the Digest when we pulled into Victoria Station. He thanked me for the book, inspected himself in the mirror, squared his shoulders and we set off down the platform together. He walked slowly, at ease, but the air was electric and I remember thinking how those lucky old pirates used to think they were hard done by walking the plank. It was obvious he wasn't going to rush through the barrier with the crowd.

As the swarming passengers thinned out before us, a flash of red told me the police were there. The pace slackened perceptibly as my eyes strained to read the situation. An R.A.F. corporal S.P. was talking to a R.A.F. Sergeant who might or might not be a policeman but wore no duty insignia. As we reached them the Sergeant stepped back and the corporal said, 'Could I see your passes'? I stepped forward reaching for my wallet but as I did so the S.W.O. let out a furious bellow.

'CORPORAL!'

'Stand to attention when you address me!'
'Call me *Sir*!'
'Do that button up!'
'You're a disgrace to the police!'
Here the sergeant butted in, 'But Sir! I am a policeman'
He was cut short.
'Are you on duty, Sergeant?'
'No, Sir.'
'Then *SHUT UP*! As for you, corporal, if I wasn't in a hurry I would march you in front of the PROVVO *NOW*. Let's go, Sarge.'
We walked together through the barrier towards the tube entrance where we parted.
'Cheerio, Sarge' he said without batting an eye.
'Good God chief!! You surely shot them down in flames!!'
'Had to Sarge. I haven't got a pass!!'

Tom Elder 1201087

Middle Wallop Tower

I'll never forget my first day as a lookout,
I'll never forget my first day on the roof,
Binoculars upon my chest with pride, I took my stand.
I gave 'em gen 'His wheels are down!' and thought 'I'm doing grand'.
The tannoy answered *'COURSE THEY ARE, THIS BASTARD'S GOING
    TO LAND'*
I'll never forget my first day on the roof.

I left the regiment to be a lookout,
I took my army 'Bulldust' on the roof,
I shook 'em all quite rigid when I gave my first salute,
There's a mark still on the lino where I stamped my army boot.
The FCO said *'CUT THAT OUT, YOU POLISH THAT, YOU COOT!'*
It's brains you want, not 'Bulldust' on the roof.

You get some binding jobs when you're a lookout,
You get some ruddy jobs up on the roof,
We do a blinking charring act right up those lousy stairs,
We wash the officers' 'How d'you do's' and swill their 'Here's and there's,
And clean up in the corner where the cat leaves his loose hairs.
You get some bastard jobs up on the roof.

But times are often slack when you're a lookout,
Sure times are often slack up on the roof.
It's rained until the blinking drome reminds you of the drink.
'Tidmarsh stand by. There's nothing up and I want forty winks,
Best lock the door. If Johnny comes, there'll be an awful stink.'
You make hay while the rain falls on the roof.

They sure encourage you when you're a lookout,
You must be bloody wizard on the roof.
You stand out in the rain till you can get no bloody wetter,
You spot a kite ten miles away, a hawk could do no better,
A WAAF pipes up *'SAY LOOKOUT. DID YOU GET THAT
    AIRCRAFT'S LETTER?'*
The answer is, 'Watch me spit off the roof'.

You sure get bags of sleep, of sleep, when you're a lookout,
There are some blissful nights up on the roof,
Old CHIPPY on the mortar shakes the teeth out of your jaws,
Old JOSE on the wander banging all the bloody doors,
Old COWELL flat out upon his back, GEE!! How that bastard snores!!
You sure get bags of sleep up on the roof.

You get some funny habits as a lookout,
Though not so funny as the folks downstairs,
Been up all night, you feel you cannot stand a minute more.
You totter round the roof and try to keep awake till four,
The tannoy shouts '*YOU RESTLESS? COME AND BASH THIS
    BLOODY FLOOR!!*'
They've got some stinking habits in control.

There's bags of grub for you when you're a lookout,
You're certainly well fed up on the roof.
The supper comes and first the duty crew all have their pick,
And even they have had it if the WAAFs turn up too slick,
For what they leave would turn a bloody salvage sorter sick.
There's bags of grub for you up on the roof.

There's bags of nice hot drinks when you're a lookout,
Life's one beverage report up on the roof,
You're dying for a drink and think you'll just pop down and see
If that old kettle's organised. It is!! Well b*!*!r me!!
You knock one back. A dame shouts '*Hell*!! That's Johnny Walker's tea'
We're nuts on FCO's up on the roof.

And since the Reverend Shepherd's been a lookout,
I've waited for this sermon on the roof,
'An Airspeed Oxford from the heavens on earth prepares to land,
The traffic on the perimeter track appears quite out of hand,
The Oxford and a lorry now have reached a better land.
So let us now all pray up on the roof'.

You've got to have *CONTROL* to be a lookout.
It's *CONTROL* that you need up on the roof.
Been up the whole night long, the blinking bombers came in hoards.
The morning dawns. '*RUN ROUND THE DROME AND CHANGE THE
    NOTICE BOARDS*'
It takes a bloody *HE-MAN* to control his vocal chords!!
Besides controlling WALLOP from the roof.

1201087 SGT. ELDER
125 WING H.Q.
2nd T.A.F.
FLYING CONTROL
MIDDLE WALLOP
1942

The Tyneside Scot

Oh Glasgow Hinny Heaven Sent,
Thoo's fund me marrit lang unkent,
Me forebears life in Scotland spent
As had forgot.
Wi' bein si lang in Durham pent
Ah've varney rot.

Here b'the Tyne's great coaly flood
A coll'ry hoose me poor abode,
An me wi' honest Scottish blood,
A Geordie was.
But thoo's forbidden me for good
The coll'ry raas.

Me Muther was a Gregor Mac,
Her 'R' rolled like a caine run slack;
If Scotland disn't git me back
Aa dee want shuttin'.
T' think a Scottie wad gan black,
Like me, hand puttin.

The Geordies leuk at me askance
When aa wad cowp for kilts me pants,
And dee for joy a hieland dance,
They caal us dottie.
But thoo seun showed them how to glance
Wi' pride on Scottie.

Yon Haggis wat thoo sent me doon
Hes torned the tyebles on the toon,
And aall tha stomachs upside doon
Te their damnation.
And aa hev won a victor's croon,
Lord o' creation.

For Geordie brags he's niver beat
And least of aall at shiftin' meat.
Tha's nowt, he says, he cannot eat,
But thoo can fettle'im.

Auld Scotland made thoo sent that geet
Big Haggis te un settl'im.

He said, 'Thar's nowt a lousy Scot
Can stomach what huz lads cannot.
Fetch me thee Haggis piping hot
Thoo brazen fella'
When only half a gob he got
His fyess went yella.

'Ye Scottish Waster!' Geordie yelled
'Tek this foul ket away te hell
Its tyest is like its rotten smell
Nee man can stand it'.
Me veins wi' Scottish blud did swell.
His spyun he handed.

'Noo Geordie hinny,' streyt Aa says,
'Wi' Scots thoo's fund thee numbe place.
Grub made to feed a mighty race
Hes knocked thoo rotten.
Watch me push Haggis through me face
Thee pride forgotten'.

'Thoo thowt a Geordie's eating cliver.
Me bait hes melted oot thee liver,
Outside a Haggis thoo'll stand niver.
Watch me chew it.
Aa'll eat Haggis sharper'n iver
Thoo can spew it.'

The spyun was like a shifter's shu'll,
And me as hungry as a bull.
In fower bites me kite was full,
The Haggis eaten.
'Noo Geordie Hinney, we's the fyul?
Thoo knaas thoo's beaten'.

And Geordie mind ye've got a neck,
Becos ya mutha couldn't byek.
Newcastle broon and stotty kyek
And singing Hinny's,
Nee'r built a fella as could tyek
A Haggis neath his pinney.

Me cap's gone for a tartan bonnet,
Me Scots pride rises like a comet,
Geordie cannot bray us from it.
Thoo's cured the braggers.
Pride cannot live abeun a *vomit*.
Thanks for the *Haggis*.

'United'

The Television's brazen voice hammered out, 'Today's Grandstand features the Second Round Cuptie between United...'.

Lucy strode to the set and snapped it off. 'Football! Football! Grown men kicking a ball about like kids!'

She collected her tea things, took them to the kitchen, got out her hat and coat, then decided not to put them on until Jon called for her.

He was cutting it a bit fine. Visiting time was in an hour and they had 30 miles to go.

She decided to wash up while she waited and when she came back to the lounge she knew they were going to be late. A black mood came over her as she remembered the last time Jon let her down and they had arrived in a ward full of visitors to an hysterical mother. Lucy would never forget the scene! Never!

Jon was a nice big happy go lucky man who lived in a permanent holiday mood, but carrying a sick mother on her back was not a holiday world and Lucy had need of a stronger support. She knew now that they were going to be late for the hospital and began to pace up and down.

'What on earth is keeping him?'

She put her hat and coat on then sat down biting the fingers of a glove. She reached out and switched on the television. The room was shattered by the roar of the football crowd. Lucy switched off and rushed from the house.

It was ten minutes' walk to Jon's but in six she was banging on his door. A faint flickering light showed from the living room but no one answered. Lucy bent down to shout in the letter box, and a distant roaring reached her ears.

'Never!' she gasped, pushing open the door. As she moved along the passage the roar reached a crescendo, she flung open the door of the

106

room. Jon was stretched out on the settee in front of the fire, a glass in his hand, the roar was deafening. United had just scored.

Jon started up, guiltily spilling his beer, Lucy switched on the room light and stabbed the screen to a shocking silence.

'So that's where you're at!' stormed Lucy. 'You great unfeeling brute! That's the sort of thing you have time for when you have no time for me! No! don't make sheep's eyes at me, you've fooled me long enough. I'm through with you Jonathan Jeremy Jones. Here's your ring back and if I see your nose again I'll slam the door on it.'

Lucy was panting with indignation and Jon didn't know what to answer. He'd been caught in the act good and proper. There was no reasoning it away, yet she had never looked so lovely to him. Her righteous wrath made her a heroic figure of blazing colour leaving him speechless. Too stricken to answer he heard the outer door bang a black finality on his gloom.

A week passed without word of Lucy and Jon felt a great need of her but lacked the will to make a move.

Saturdays had always been a full happy day, the trip to Bedford to see Lucy's mother, the meal in town, the pictures and home again – but that was all finished.

He fell back into the old routine. He could now follow United and on Saturday he got out the car and set off for the match. As he approached the railway station he was surprised to see the crowds moving in the wrong direction. Three red and white scarved chaps waved him down. He recognised his old cronies Nick, Buster and Elliot.

'Going to the match Jon?' 'United's got to win this one.' 'No trains running!' 'Bloody railwaymen.' 'Packed the bird in Jon?' The car was suddenly filled with cigarette smoke, boisterous laughter and a nostalgia that Jon was not too sure he wanted. The old routine of the match, the pub crawl, the fish and chips and the punch up at the disco.

As they approached the station the dispersing crowd slowed them down. Among the red and white favours a yellow coated figure stood out in contrast.

'We've got time for a pint Buster.' 'Pull in Jon.' 'What, thirsty already Elliot?'

On impulse, Jon swung into the Railway Arms. 'Everybody out!' he bawled and when they were out he shouted, 'Sorry fella's, it's all off. I've got to go back for something.'

Amazed the three musketeers watched him do a smart U turn and shoot back up the Station Road.

He soon caught up with the forlorn figure in the yellow coat.

Lucy turned as he rolled down the window, flashing beautiful eyes then covering them with a blank look.

'Lucy, we can't talk here. I'll take you to the hospital.' He stepped out and reached for her arm. She backed off and some passers by stopped to watch. 'Come on Lucy, we can't talk here.'

'You can't park here either,' said a warden. Lucy gave in. 'All right then, turn up Queen Street.'

The fragrance of Lucy swept over Jon and he couldn't believe the world could transform itself in so short a time.

'Lucy, I'm sorry about last week; the trains aren't running and I'd be pleased to run you to the Hospital.'

'I wasn't going to the Hospital, Jon.'

Jon sobered; stopped the car and turned to Lucy. 'Mam?' he said not wanting to commit his fears to words, and putting an arm round her shoulder.

'She's better Jon. She came home on Thursday and is staying at Daisy's.'

'Where were you going off to, Lucy?'

'I was going to the match Jon. I just hoped we might . . . we could be, you know ---- UNITED.'

Tulips from Amsterdam

Many of you will have forgotten Pieter van der Groot, the boy hero of Holland who saved Amsterdam from inundation by plugging a leaking sea wall with his arm. I became his friend in later life through our mutual interest as bulb growers and among a few of his effects that came to me was a letter to be opened five years after his parents' death. That time has now passed and I can throw a strange and new light on the dark secret he carried through life, when the world revered him as the saviour of his city.

You have only to recall the headlines about his exploit to know what a fantastic halo was fixed around his head by the nation, as he lay in a coma for a fortnight, frozen to the lips after lying with his arm thrust into the dam through a whole winter's night.

'Boy loses his rabbit and saves a city.'

'Two Lips' de Groot saves Amsterdam.'

Pieter survived and awoke to find himself a legend. His High Church parents had practically canonised him and every detail of that night was already history of how he went out to feed his rabbit late and never returned. He was found frozen on the sea wall. Only his two lips were moving, framing the word 'Amsterdam. Amsterdam. Amster dam.'

Holland prayed for the whole of that fortnight.

'*Dear Tom*' the letter reads '*Here is something I must get off my conscience. Something my dear father and mother would not have understood. My rabbit was in the hutch that winter's night but my sister Gretchen's damned Hamster jumped out and disappeared into the dark. All I remember is reaching into a hole, getting my arm stuck and cursing that damned hamster, damned hamster, damned hamster.*'

Leather Helmets

Life is a tale of a man and his moods
The greatest of which is Love,
Least so the poets tell us, all of which just goes to prove
That poets never marry or they'd blowed soon think again,
For the sunshine of this love stuff after marriage turns to rain.

But to begin our story – You've heard sentimentalists rave
Of that greater love of man for man, like Jonathan and Dave,
Laurel and Hardy, Cole and Coke, there's Crosse and Blackwell too,
But there's a modern version that is stranger though it's true.

Here is a love as real as the proverbial love of Mike,
The love of an ancient mangle for another motorbike.
The owners are mere details but their story can be read
In this saga of an Aggie and a Calthorpe overhead.

Once there was upon a time, a Mac and Mac's are thrifty,
Who owned a noble steed, a Calthorpe O.H.V. 350.
He tuned it like a fiddle till sixty nine was ease,
He is a scion of those knights with pots between their knees.

As long as leather helmets hurtle on the dusty roads
Mac and his Cal will stand for shortest time and biggest loads.
The feats of that 350 would run me short of page,
She was a blinking triumph of efficiency at age.

Now Cal once had a stranger on his pew, who'd sat behind
Of Mac and marvelled at the rev. and shick without a grind,
And when he tried himself and on the Fell went for a hop
Old Cal had shed some bitter tears before he was in top.

Once there, old Cal just settled down to show this clumsy fellow
That Pictree isn't thirty second run from Portobello.
He stuck his head behind the lamp and took hold with his knees,
'This is the life for me!' he cried. 'I like this homemade breeze.'

110

You've heard about the race between the Tortoise and the Weasel
The modern version could involve a light weight Coventry Eangle.
'I'm through with this,' the hombre said, 'Mac lead me to a bike.'
And that's how Cal got a lady pal, Old Aggie, where's her like?
'Just kick her up now, mister, she'll shift a bit I guess.'
I kicked the crank then came the sound of cannons going off.
'She'll do,' I cried. 'She seems to have a fairly healthy cough.'

She'll take some keeping on the road, that fella cannot hold her,
'I'll take her home alright,' said Mac, 'just fake that licence holder'.
And Aggie hurtled homewards, having got the total works,
And even then her Conrod was a thing for drawing corks.

Old Pictree heard afar off a strange unusual humming
That deepened to a roar to herald Aggie's first home coming.
That farmyard knew velocities unconnected with a farmer,
The big spill came the day we held the Whitsuntide Gymkana.

Imagine just a mile of straight set with giant trees,
And Cal without a pipe on doing seventy with ease,
A naked rider lying down his body in a cramp,
Then Mac was on his stomach and old Cal stood on his lamp.

Those were the days when 'XL' was a substitute for 'R'.
Till Aggie's piston grabbed the pot with such an awful jar.
The rider's face went blank and then his ears began to tingle,
Instead of Aggie's usual cough she just went 'Yingle Yingle'.

Re-booked, she hit the road again and did things rather better,
To Langdon Beck with just two gears and half a carburettor.
And later Cal performed this feat and scaled the Swinhope Top,
Two up – and up – and up on the grass and never missed a pop.

But coming back as to the Folly 'straight' we crouched and flew,
The axle in the back wheel folded neatly into two.
So Mac just screwed the broken bits up inside the cone
And Cal's record's unbroken, he sees you safely home.

Once Cal and Aggie hit the trail for Ripon on the Booze,
With a Beezer man (Mac's sister was the ballast he did use).
They grabbed 'handfuls' of throttle, the Beezer set the pace,
But Aggie grabbed her pot and so was left out of the race.

The Beezer forced the pace and people heard the beat,
As Cal two up and flat out just screamed down Watling Street.
And coming home the Beezer's pace at last did swift diminish,
The piston folded up and only Cal was left to finish.

This second siege of Aggie's made the owner swear to sell her,
But Aggie with a new pot on was quite a different fella.
And so she took the road again much to Mac's disgust,
For Aggie's constitution oft had him in the dust.

My parents once cut down to size an old four poster bed,
Some hefty lengths of brass bound pipe were thrown out in the shed.
'Bags I,' MacGregor said on sight, he was a covetous type.
'Imagine what a BOOM 'twill have stuck on my EXHAUST PIPE.'

Strange ends oft come to things but this has all the rest on toast,
Just think of the outraged feelings of that ancient corner post.
Oft as my parents slumbered, its silent watch t'would keep,
Its thund'ring round the country now destroying people's sleep.

That upswept can of Cal's had got a most terrific cough,
Especially when he's screaming and the holder slackens off.
I've seen him stop in High Street, I've heard his brake drums squeal,
His engine 'coughing' open port, the flames past his front wheel.

Aggie's favourite 'noise' was like the bark of sliding dogs,
He carried his tools in the gear box and it altered some of the cogs.
And Cal's Horn Bulb came off a Ford, the reed from Lor' knows where,
Would play anything from a bank note to the Londonderry Air.

But all good things come to an end and bad ones do as well.
Old Aggie seized her pot again, the rider shouted 'Hell!'.
They were coming back from Felton, an uneventful run,
When on the Morpeth 'straight' old Aggie wouldn't take the gun.

Ten times the oil pump answered, at least it's ten I think.
And when the last she fired, you couldn't stand the pen and ink.
The plug was oiled and Aggie's cough was just a lot of 'spurts'
As though she ran on Mother Siegel's Syrup or Tiger Nuts.

'Old Aggie's got a faulty plug,' I said, Mac wasn't pleased.
Quoth he, 'I know those symptoms, she's gone and went and seized.'
We tied two scarves together and Cal took up his load,
Old Aggie came her last on tow along the Buxfield Road.

I knew I'd have to sell her, cause Mac put his foot down.
'That (noun)' quoth he 'with blood on done orter be put down.'
And so he got another pot and a really decent plug,
I ran her in at fifty and then ran in a 'MUG'.
So ends an epic friendship, Aggie gone, old Cal retires.
She's standing in the shed there with a couple of brand new tyres.
The rust creeps o'er the bed post never more to roam,
He's got a pain in the Maggie since he towed his Aggie home.

To credit all that Calthorpe's feats, they just had to be seen,
I've seen it take a chicken and pluck it really clean.
That hen ran from a farmyard, the Calthorpe gave a hoot,
It did three revs with Mac's front wheel and came out like a coot.

Up north there winds a wondrous road to Cresswell by the sea,
And often at the weekends those mangles you would see,

Chasing each other on the straight and taking corners blind,
And strewing lines of camping outfit, tools and things behind.

And once they reached the seashore but half an hour from dark
And Aggie's battery was lost, she wouldn't show a spark.
'That's jiggered it,' the natives said, 'You cannot get home now.'
But ere they spoke, two puffs of smoke shot over Cresswell Brow.

On, on, they fled, two idiots, flat out to beat the sun,
And never will the memory fade that I have of that run,
Old Aggie stood up like a trump and close behind her roar
Came Mac, half poisoned with her fumes, but none the less full bore.

What BEDLAM came to BEDLINGTON. Oh, DINNINGTON the DIN.
They couldn't see them coming or they must have run 'em in.
Ten miles to go, on, on they pressed into the fading night,
And never did more hideous roar cut through a Sunday Night.

'Tis still retold the Parson said, 'My friends, oh peace be still.'
Just as those dogs were swapping cogs, to climb up Sherriff Hill
And as the great crescendo burst upon the town,
The people shot into the street in case the Church fell down.

Policemen shook their truncheons, the steeple shook with bells.
The Parson shook his fist and queried, 'What the bloody 'ell?'
The Curate not to be outdone shook them even more,
Shouting to the deaf old Verger, 'Can't you shut that bloody door?'

Old Aggie's pot was luminous, the flames shot two feet clear,
On corners Cally's 'pop-back' was beautiful to hear.
For Mac was putting off no time, his blood began to boil
Each time that Aggie shut off, she anointed him with oil.

And when at last they stood astride their mangles smoking hot,
And lit a fag to celebrate, they lit them on the pot.
'We averaged forty five, old bean, to Heaton it appears.'
And Lor your bloomin 'pop-back' – music in the sinner's ears.

And if you take hold of the horn and press it carefully
Old Cal will give a mournful cry, 'Aggie come back to me.'
And next year even Cal and Mac, the best of friends, must part,
'Cause Cal has got a broken frame, or is it a broken heart?

And if you go up that white road that leads to Peter's Gate,
It's maybe changed a bit and been brought up to date.
The ghostly traffic passes through under new control
They've got a blinking Robot up and Peter's on the Dole.

Just hunt about until you find the Angels' Auto Club,
Or maybe Dave and Jonathan come flying from a pub,
And fold their wings and ride away, they're still the best of pals,
And Dave is riding Aggie and Jonathan's on Cal.

Eighton Banks 1953

Icing Sugar

John looked aghast at the paper bag. He'd just put it down on the snow while he threw some stones on the frozen pond and when he picked it up the bottom fell out and all the sugar spilled on to the snow.

'What would Mam say??!!'

Stricken he read aloud from the broken packet, 'SILVER SPOON, Icing Sugar for decoration, store in a dry place.' You're telling me!

He scrabbled the small heap of sugar together. It was all one with the snow. 'Hopeless! Damn Sugar!'

He threw away the packet and kicked the heap into oblivion – tears of frustration in his eyes.

He could hear again Mam shouting from the kitchen, 'Johnny, Johnny. Quick son, take this' (she thrust a pound coin in his hand) 'and run and get a bag of Icing Sugar, don't forget, ICING SUGAR, it's special. They said they'd have some more today.'

He could feel the coin dancing up and down in his trouser pocket as he ran down the street.

'Come on Johnny,' his pals shouted from the frozen pond as he passed. 'It's hard enough to slide on.'

'OK. When I come back,' he yelled over his shoulder running faster still, and leaping up the steps, as the automatic doors opened, swallowing him into the crush of Saturday morning shoppers.

There was a buzz of housewives at the icing sugar. He seized a packet and ran to the quick check-out.

'Fifty two pence change, young man.'

He was off – down the stairs and away up the village. The boys were still testing the ice.

Johnny seized a big stone and flung it high above the pond. The ice sang, but no cracks appeared. He slid gingerly out to the middle and stamped his feet, jumping up and down then slid confidently to the far side, then round the edge to the group, shouting 'Come on kids, it's OK; I'll be back in a minute.'

He turned to the sugar bag, the boys laughed as the sugar spilled out.

'Cor Johnny, you're not half going to cop it.'

He turned away in his misery, towards home but the nearer he got the closer gripped the horns of his dilemma.

Suddenly his mind was made up – he made a detour to avoid his pals and ran back to the store.

He would get another bag of sugar for Mam.

There was only one bag left. As he seized it, a white coated assistant said, 'D'you want a basket, son?'

'This is all I want,' said Johnny, flushing violently and scurried away.

Seeing the busy check-outs he moved with a group selecting empty boxes, popped his sugar in one and moved down past the waiting queue, to the automatic exit.

A few persons were waiting about the door. One was replacing a wall telephone.

In his haste Johnny reached for the non-existent door handles but the doors refused to open. He pushed. Nothing happened. He turned in panic. A tall man said 'Just wait a minute.' They stood together, Johnny clutching his box. Someone appeared outside the door and suddenly it opened.

Johnny galloped out and the man outside hurried after him.

In the car park the man caught up with him. 'I have reason to believe you have goods unpaid for, young man.'

'I paid for it. I paid for it.'

He broke down as he was led back to the store. 'My Mam's waiting for it for the cake.'

In the office a stern lady took him by the shoulder, looked in his eyes and asked 'Did you pay for it, sonny?'

'I did. I did. My Mam gave me a pound to get it.'

'Did you get any change?'

'Yes, it's here in my pocket.'

He fumbled out the coins and put them in her hand. A small slip of paper fell to the floor.

She picked it up, read it and handed it to the man.

'Off you go, son. Sorry to have given you this trouble.'

The Scientific Age

Oh men of science stand ye forth
And show to me
The worth of all your great ant industry;
Your delving
in the earth
and sea
and sky
and mind
and all your clever findings.
Answer me.
Where stand we now?
The blind led by the blinding.

Devotees of the brazen brain
Ye scions of the smart.
Ye pursuers of logic
Ye Scorners of the heart.
The Chemist
In his omniscience
Is poisoning our food;
The Doctor
With his wonder drug
Lies buried
'neath the flood of addicts;
Psychiatrists.
The 'mind experts'
Are suicides top Score.
Oh clever generation,
What are you
Looking for?

Life giving oxygen by which we live
And breathe and move and work,
The Jumbo Jet will burn eight tons

To fly you to New York.
Albeit nature's spreading woods
Recharge the air again,
Bi-products of our industry
Kill these with acid rain.
Behold the simple aerosol
To kill the humble fly,
Is eating up the stratosphere
Which guards us in the skies.
The vultures of disaster
On Hiroshima we loosed,
In what colossal magnitude will
They come home to roost?

The sculptor,
Lost in abstract,
Creating something new,
Discovers
On the seashore
That every kipper knew.
The artist
Blind to beauty
Must paint
What can't be seen

Must poets
Follow
This sad trail?
Till words no longer mean
That man
Communicates
With man
Across deception's mist?
That heart to heart
Can call
Shake hands
Instead of fists?

If
Life
And love
And truth were given
To mankind to enjoy
For Christ's sake hear what Jesus said:
The Nazarene boy foretold
The gift of life divine
Could not be reconciled
With any way of living.
But that of a little child.

HIS WORDS REVEALED HE UNTO BABES
THOUGH HIDDEN FROM THE WISE,
SO SIMPLE ARE HIS STATEMENTS
WE CAN'T BELIEVE OUR EYES.
THE KINGDOM OF HEAVEN'S WITHIN YOU
SEEK AND YE SHALL FIND.
ASK AND T'WILL BE GIVEN
BY THE ONE ETERNAL MIND.
BEFORE YOU CALL, HE WILL ANSWER,
KNOCK AND HE'LL OPEN THE DOOR,
THE KINGDOM OF HEAVEN'S WITHIN YOU.
WHAT ON EARTH ARE YOU WAITING FOR?

Forgetfulness

One of the disabilities that smite a man coming up for 70 is the occasional lapse of memory, and the consequences in a fast moving world could be so far reaching that it becomes fascinating to pursue one such lapse to its logical conclusion.

My wife is very kind about this. The other day she said,

'Tom, I do believe you've forgotten my name.'

'Of course I have. Why do you suppose I've been calling you 'Darling' for the last two years?'

My wife is also very indulgent, and seeing me admire something in a shop window is enough to make her bring out all her housekeeping money.

'Go on,' she said 'Go mad.'

So I bought the leather coat in Peter Percy's, walked out straight over the Marlowes, put in in the car, forgot the mirror and pulled out right under a 302 bus.

The gate opened and a nice old chap beckoned me in.

'I'm Peter,' he said.

'How do you do, Mr Percey?' I said.

'SAINT PETER' he said. 'HE wants to see you. You're late'.

I was ushered into the Presence.

'I came as soon as I could' I said. 'I put my foot down. Do you like my coat?'

God said 'In my book it says, "Take no thought for what you put on".'

'Ah, well' I said, 'if it's like that I may as well take it off.'

God said, 'You are forgetting yourself, Elder.'

I looked down, I was naked and my black toenail stood out against the white marble like a brass button in a coal cellar or somewhere, I forget where.

119

God said, 'How did he come?'
Peter said, 'In a 1960 Morris Oxford, Sir.'
God said, '1960!! Has it been inspected?'
Peter said, 'Not yet, Sir. St. Christopher is on duty up the M1.'
God said, 'Send somebody else.'
Peter looked round and said, 'Gabrielle would you be so kind?'
'Certainly, Sir,' said Gabrielle bowing low and running from the hall.
Came the sound of a car door opening and shutting and the horn started to blare out like the last trump.
God put his fingers in his ears.
Peter opened a window and shouted 'Gabby, this is not your day.'
The noise stopped but the echoes rumbled away into eternity.
'Sorry, Sir,' said Peter, 'Gabrielle has a thing about horns.'
Gabrielle entered submissively.
God said, 'Well, Gabrielle?'
'MOT ran out last month, Sir.'
'I forgot, Sir,' I burst in but they ignored me.
God looking out the window said 'Back springs gone, Gabrielle?'
'Possibly not, Sir. The boot is heavily laden.'
'Laden with what, Gabrielle?'
'Crates of home brewed beer, Sir.'
God said, 'Is it yours, Elder?'
'Yes, Sir' I said. 'In your book it says, "Take no thought for what you drink".'
Peter said 'We have a right one here, Sir.'
Gabrielle said 'I think he's a wrong'un, Sir.'
God waved me dismissed. 'Show him round, Gabrielle.'
I followed Gabrielle. The door clanged with horrible finality.
We went downstairs.
He opened another.
'This is the boiler room' he said.
'Blimey, I didn't know you had central heating!'
'Get in there,' he said.
'Blimey,' I said 'It's hot in here.'
'You can have overalls' said Gabrielle and suddenly I had my leather coat on.
'It's hellish hot!' I shouted.
'Yes,' said Gabrielle, 'You're posted on the two till ten shift.'
The door clanged behind him like the sound of doom and the wall of coal slid down and covered my black toe nail.

I looked up the enormous chimney and there was the face of God, sad but kind.

'One favour, Sir.'

'SPEAK,' He said.

'Send me down a crate of my home brew.'

'Granted,' he said.

And as I kneeled to thank him, I bruised my knee on the crate coming up out of the coal.

I knocked the neck off on the furnace door and drank deeply.

It tasted like death. The face of God was still kind.

'You forgot to put the yeast in, Elder.'

1946

Over 80

Age is a quality of mind.
If you have left your dreams behind,
If hope is cold,
If you no longer plan ahead,
If ambitions all are dead,
Then you are old.
But if you make of life the best,
If in your life you still have zest,
If LOVE you hold,
No matter how the years go by
No matter how the birthdays fly
You are not old.

AUTHOR UNKNOWN

I get bored with football games,
Some blokes only talk of dames
And I can't abide the ones who do the horses,
But the bloke who makes me sick,
Really gets upon my wick,
Is the old man who still lives back in the forces.

That is why I've got no friends.
Every day the good Lord sends
Someone says, 'You used 'ter *What*? Don't make me laugh.'
Please don't all go away,
With your leave I want to say
Just a few words on the old days in the RAF.

I was in flying Control
When the Spits did Victory Rolls,
I cold tell you of some WIZARD PRANG adventures.
But *now* its quite a feat

Just to get up off my seat
And try to keep control upon my dentures.

The boys will tell you of the jars
And the lines we shot in bars,
And where the heck did we put all those bitters?
Now I drop my hearing aid
In my glass of lemonade
And I can't even hear the ladies' titters.

Do you recall the dances
How we longed for the chances
to get up with the girl that we had dated?
Now they just go and come,
All you need is just a bum
And the blinking room to get up and rotate it.

Can you recall again
Sneaking home at half past ten
With a prayer that Dad and Mam were fast asleep?
Now a car roars in the night
And when I switch on the light
Someone says, 'Cor, look, we've waked up your old creep.'

Each weekend we would start
Shopping down the old town Mart
With our few bobs we'd bargain and we'd bicker.
Now it's 'Take yer hands off Dad.' 'Take the good uns with the bad.'
'Arf a pahnd Ma. That'll cost you just a Nicker'.

Just a ride there in the bus
Was a holiday for us.
'Two returns, Sir? Yes. That's seven pence to pay.'
Now it really makes me sad,
'Get your finger out, Grandad!
You old codgers fink I've got all bleedin' day.'

Do you still travel down the ways
Of your old courting days?
Shakespeare's right! for all the world still loves a lover.
Does love still bring you the chance
To relive your old romance?
Does it take you nearly three weeks to recover?

After forty years have passed
Women just don't age so fast –
Take my wife – she's going to kill me if I mention her –
Well, the lady sitting next,
Said, 'I never would have guessed
You'd be married to that poor old CHELSEA PENSIONER!'

Age is a quality of mind,
If you have left your dreams behind,
If hope is cold,
If you no longer plan ahead,
If ambitions all are dead,
Then you are old.
But if you make of life the best,
If in your life you still have zest,
If LOVE you hold,
No matter how the years go by
No matter how the birthdays fly
You are not old.

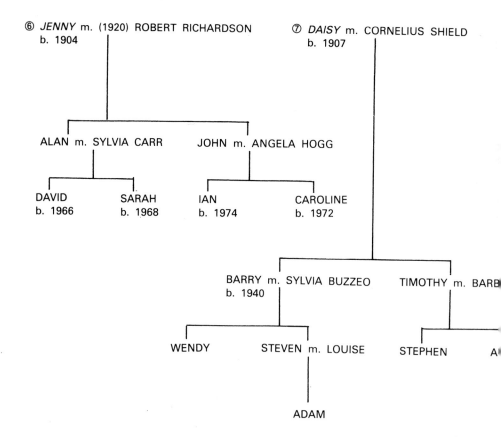

⑥ *JENNY* m. (1920) ROBERT RICHARDSON
b. 1904

⑦ *DAISY* m. CORNELIUS SHIELD
b. 1907

ALAN m. SYLVIA CARR

JOHN m. ANGELA HOGG

DAVID
b. 1966

SARAH
b. 1968

IAN
b. 1974

CAROLINE
b. 1972

BARRY m. SYLVIA BUZZEO
b. 1940

TIMOTHY m. BARB

WENDY

STEVEN m. LOUISE

STEPHEN

A

ADAM